THE
TOUR

THE TOUR

RUPERT GUINNESS

BEHIND THE SCENES OF CADEL EVANS'
TOUR DE FRANCE

hardie grant books
MELBOURNE · LONDON

SBS

An SBS Book

Published in 2012 by Hardie Grant Books
Hardie Grant Books (Australia)
Ground Floor, Building 1
658 Church Street
Richmond, Victoria 3121
www.hardiegrant.com.au

Hardie Grant Books (UK)
Dudley House, North Suite
34–35 Southampton Street
London WC2E 7HF
www.hardiegrant.co.uk

Copyright © Rupert Guinness 2012
A Cataloguing-in-Publication entry is available from the catalogue of the National
Library of Australia at www.nla.gov.au
ISBN: 9781742703855

Cover design by Design by Committee
Text design by Peter Daniel
Typeset by Kirby Jones
Colour reproduction by Splitting Image Colour Studio
Printed and bound in Australia by Griffin Press

To Ian Fuge ...
for backing me when it mattered

CONTENTS

FOREWORD

I will be the first to admit my first impression of Cadel Evans was probably not all that great. I know a lot of the riders in the peloton. It's hard not to when you've been racing professionally for nearly 20 years. We ride alongside each other for hours at a time, day after day. We tough it out in the cruellest of conditions. Sometimes, in the classics, it is pedalling through pouring rain and bone-chilling cold. In July and August, it is suffering through hours in the saddle in choking heat. We drag our bodies up and over some of the steepest mountain passes, ones that even cars have trouble negotiating. These shared experiences through the toughest of conditions build a common bond …

But it wasn't like that for me when it came to Cadel.

Sure, we would exchange a few pleasantries at the start of races. Sometimes we would even say a few things to each other mid-race. But I didn't know him that well. We were never teammates until he came to the BMC racing team at the start of the 2010 season.

He was a rider who came across in the press as a bit uptight and fairly introverted. What I didn't know back then was that this quietness and the 'I'm better off alone' image came from a meticulous focus on racing his bicycle to the best of his ability.

I came to discover after two seasons of being his teammate that bicycle racing is what consumes him. He studies course maps for hours. He analyses the width of roads, looks at the elevations of all the big climbs and even researches potential wind directions. He's one of those guys who need to know every detail of every race they ride. And that intense focus is often mistaken for unfriendliness or even rudeness. It couldn't be further from the truth.

I vividly remember the first meeting I had with Cadel, when we were trying to lure him to BMC. It happened in a hotel right outside of Zurich, two weeks after he won the world road championship in Mendrisio, Switzerland, in the autumn of 2009.

Before riding away from all the world's best cyclists to secure his first rainbow jersey, Cadel was considered the guy who was always in position to win, but never able to deliver. That was a bit of my read on him heading into our first face-to-face meeting.

It seemed to me that this would likely be the final contract Cadel would sign in a career that began with mountain biking in the 1990s. Team management and I thought he would find the rapidly growing, upstart BMC team to be a good fit in the twilight of his career.

Expectations were relatively low for the squad, which was still one step below the upper echelon of professional cycling teams.

So, as we engaged in conversation before dinner that night, I told him, 'I think you're really going to like this team. Och [BMC team president Jim Ochowicz] and [main sponsor] Andy Rihs are stand-up guys. I really believe I can help you podium at the Tour de France'.

No sooner had I said that did he look me dead in the eye and say three sentences that will stick with me forever: 'I've already done that. I've podiumed two times at the Tour. I want to win it', he said matter-of-factly.

Talk about a jaw-dropper. There I was thinking: 'This guy's 33 years old and he wants to win the world's greatest race?' I wasn't so sure. In fact, I hadn't even thought about it. But the look he gave me, and the way he told me what he wanted, was deeply convincing.

Flash-forward to the eve of the final time trial in the 2011 Tour de France to get a true sense of what a consummate professional and amazing man Cadel Evans really is.

For nearly three weeks, my teammates and I had done everything possible to keep him within reach of the lead. We shepherded him around crashes that knocked out several favourites. Some days we set the pace on the front, hour after hour, to send the message that Cadel rightly had a place with the top contenders. But with only a 42.5-kilometre time trial to race, and a 53-second deficit to make up, it would be solely on Cadel's shoulders.

Our time to help him was done. He would be completely on his own. And that made all of us nervous as heck. So as we prepared for dinner, few words were spoken. I doubt I was the only one feeling the tension in the room.

What changed everything was Cadel's demeanour that night as we sat around the table. The nine of us shared a glass of wine and Cadel chatted it up as if a training ride lay ahead the next day, not the most important race of his life. Here he was, going through his routine as if it were any other day. It was almost as if he had gone over that scenario a million times in his head. It really showed me how much he'd grown and how much he had changed.

The rider I once regarded as individualistic and not anything about a team was subtly reassuring us all that he could finish the job. It left me feeling proud, honoured and amazed—all at the same time.

It's staggering to think I've had more than 400 teammates over the years, and that nine times I have helped a team-mate win the world's greatest race. But my most memorable ride into the streets of Paris with a Tour champion beside me was certainly with Cadel.

To watch him make the transition from Tour de France contender to Tour de France champion was impressive. All those hours of poring over race maps, countless hours and kilometres of training, and that singular focus finally paid off.

It brings a big smile to my face when I think how different my first impression of him is to the man and friend I've come to know.

Thanks for the memories, Cadel.

George Hincapie
June 2012

Hincapie has started in an equal record of 16 Tours de France with Dutchman Joop Zoetemelk, and if picked for the 2012 edition will become the outright record holder.

He is also the only rider to race in nine Tour-winning teams— with Lance Armstrong (1999–2005), Alberto Contador (2007) and Cadel Evans (2011).

Very HAPPY BIRTHDAY
MICHAEL
I thought that you would
be interested in reading
Rupert's book. Have a
very good day on the 18th
Lots of love
R.

1

TURNING THE PAGE: JOINING BMC

On 24 July 2011 Cadel Evans and his teammates were in a Paris nightclub celebrating his victory several hours earlier in the Tour de France. The presentations and speeches were over; the meal was eaten. Champagne had made way for fine wine. Some of the riders, having seemingly forgotten their exhaustion after racing for three weeks, joined their partners and guests on the dance floor; others mingled at the bar recounting tales of triumph and torture.

The gathering at Le 1515—a *boîte de nuit* in Paris's eighth arrondissement that is often frequented by celebrities—was not the only one celebrating Cadel's breakthrough win, which saw him, as leader of the American-registered BMC team, beat the Luxembourg brothers Andy and Fränk Schleck, leaving them to finish second and third overall. Post-Tour parties were being held everywhere. In Australia, half a world away, a record audience of 704,000 people had tuned into SBS Television into the early hours of Monday morning to watch the final day of racing, and Cadel's win was being celebrated as arguably the greatest individual sporting feat ever by an Australian.

Those celebrations began several hours earlier, as soon as Cadel crossed the finish line of the 3470-kilometre Tour's

21st stage on the cobblestoned Champs Elysées on a balmy, sun-struck summer afternoon. A Tour finish is always celebrated, but this one—the first by an Australian—was special. After years of speculation about the Tour's credibility, at long last the feeling was that the race had a fully deserving winner.

And that winner was Cadel, who took the yellow jersey from Andy Schleck in the 42-kilometre individual time trial in Grenoble the day before and who, at the age of 34, was the oldest winner in 88 years.

It was Cadel who was feted as the champion as he stood atop the podium against the backdrop of the Arc de Triomphe with an Australian flag draped over his shoulders. And it was to Cadel that Paris-based Australian singer Tina Arena sang the national anthem, 'Advance Australia Fair'; she'd dreamt the night before that she sang at the Tour jersey presentation, and she'd made herself available when she woke up.

It was also Cadel who was cheered by thousands of fans—many of them Australian—who flocked to watch the Tour finale.

This was the same Cadel who many—riders, media and cycling aficionados—had written off as not having what it takes to win the Tour. Even the Belgian great and five-time Tour winner Eddy Merckx doubted Cadel's ability to win the world's biggest bike race. Only six months earlier, Merckx said of Cadel:

He has a good team. The structure is good. Everyone will ride for him. But I don't know if he can beat Schleck, Contador,

Basso, Kreuziger, Nibali and Sagan. I hope for him, but it will not be easy. At 33, to compete against riders who are 25 or 26 is not so easy; but he is still a champion. For sure.

By the time the 2011 Tour reached its crescendo in the Alps, however, and was settled in the Grenoble time trial, Merckx had nothing but praise for Cadel. A lot is said about athletes in the public eye, but when someone like Merckx speaks, you tend to listen. When he suggested that Cadel was too old to be a top Tour contender in 2011, Cadel would have disagreed, and with good reason: he is now not only the youngest rider to win a mountain bike World Cup at 20 years of age but, at the other end of his career, the oldest rider to win the Tour since 1923.

But on this July night in Paris, hours after his win, no-one's doubts mattered. It was a time to celebrate.

Cadel arrived at Le 1515 wearing jeans and his Tour winner's yellow jersey—*le maillot jaune.* He was met by standing applause from 300 guests who had long since begun the revelry, and it was clear he was still trying to absorb the impact of the moment he came to a stop on the Champs Elysées and his jubilant teammates leapt on top of him.

As the applause continued, it would not have been lost on Cadel that 12 months earlier he had been at exactly the same place—Le 1515—and had been met by an equally warm ovation from the same gathering of BMC staff, family and supporters. Despite the disappointment in finishing 26th overall in the 2010 Tour, they had all been keen to celebrate BMC's first participation in the Tour—it was then still a second-division ProContinental team—and Cadel's one day in the yellow jersey (which had been stymied by the fracture of his elbow in a crash in stage 8). The big difference in 2011, besides his win, was that he finally got to race a Tour without the misfortune of past bids, such as those he encountered in 2008 and 2010 when crashes ruined his Tour.

• • •

In 2009 Cadel left the Silence-Lotto team to join BMC, which was then racing in the United States but was intent on racing in the top league after recruiting former Italian world champion Alessandro Ballan, Dutchman Karsten Kroon, and American George Hincapie, who had ridden for Lance Armstrong in all of his seven Tour wins and for Contador in 2009.

BMC team president Ochowicz, a former Olympic speed skater and cyclist, has steered some of world cycling's most adventurous projects. He cut his teeth creating the American 7-Eleven team, which began racing the US circuit and then went to Europe in 1985 to race the classics and grand tours. It became a major player over its seven-year existence, highlighted by Andy Hampsten's win—the first by an American—in the 1988 Giro d'Italia. When 7-Eleven ended its sponsorship, the team rode under the banner of Motorola, which was wanting to expand its brand in Europe. One of its biggest recruits was another Australian in Tour legend, and idol to a young Cadel, Phil Anderson, who quickly left his imprint with a number of early wins and a 1991 Tour stage victory.

Tony Rominger, Cadel's European agent, laid the path that led Cadel to the BMC team. Rominger had put the idea to BMC owner Andy Rihs that with a rider like Cadel, BMC would be well positioned to gain a wildcard entry to the 2010 Tour de France. Cadel still had a year on his contract with Silence-Lotto, but the discussions began.

At the time, Cadel was focused on the annual world road championships that were to be held in Mendrisio, Switzerland. From the day he first learned of the course and then saw it, he knew it was tailor-made for him; and the fact that it was only 3 kilometres from his home and friends and family in Stabio provided added motivation.

His race preparation had been meticulous. By the time the world titles came, Cadel knew every metre of the 262-kilometre circuit—the danger points to be alert for, and when to attack.

However, he was still keen to settle on his future after the world titles—that surety would give him the added calm heading into the big race. Cadel wanted to know that ahead of him was a team that would not only support him but could also build a structure around him and develop him. Hence he was eager to meet with Ochowicz before the title—and he did, at the Australian team hotel in Varese, near the Swiss border in Italy.

Ochowicz was initially reluctant to have a meeting the day before the race, because he didn't want to disturb Cadel. He had no way of knowing that the meeting would actually provide Cadel with enormous peace of mind, but Cadel's sense of confidence was evident in his race the next day.

After finding himself in the decisive group with 255 kilometres of racing behind him, he seized upon a moment of hesitation among his rivals, changed gears and attacked and rode away alone over the last 7 kilometres, driven by only one thing: the desire to win.

Cadel refused to look behind once he set off. He had to block out thoughts of anything that could take his imminent victory away from him in the dying kilometres—someone counterattacking, catching and passing him; a mechanical problem, such as a puncture; or cramping or any other physical problem.

He continued like that to the very end, through the phalanx of cheering people and up the final drag to the finish, where he crossed the line first. Incredibly to many observers, he did so with the most modest of victory salutes—a gentle raise of his right hand and kiss of his fingertips.

Before the eyes of the cycling world—from his loyal supporters and fans to his detractors—Cadel had proven that he was a real winner. And just how much it really meant to Cadel was clear as he stood on the podium, flanked by second-placed Alexandr Kolobnev of Russia and third-placed Joaquim Rodríguez of Spain, in the prestigious world champion's rainbow jersey that he would wear in every road race for the next year.

For Ochowicz the result was bittersweet at first. As much as he was happy for Cadel, he feared that the victory might be the death knell of BMC's bid to secure him, considering how much the world title would have increased his value on the market.

Ochowicz's concern was unfounded. When he telephoned Cadel later that day to say congratulations, Cadel reassured him that the deal was still on. And in November, Cadel signed with BMC.

With Cadel's signing, the BMC team gained the stature to be invited to the big races in Europe as a wildcard. Then, to everyone's astonishment, within 18 months BMC had transformed from being a small US-based outfit into a celebrated Tour-winning team—just as Cadel had transformed, from being a rider who many thought had squandered his chances and was past his prime, into a celebrated Tour champion.

• • •

Cadel's 26th place overall in the 2010 Tour de France, at 50 minutes 27 seconds to Spaniard Alberto Contador, came after he crashed 7 kilometres into the 189-kilometre stage 8 from Station des Rousses in the Jura mountains to Morzine-Avoriaz in the Alps. On the fateful day of the crash, as joyous as it must have been to receive the yellow jersey, his pain on the following rest day, when he discovered he had fractured his left elbow, was a worrying precursor to what awaited him when the Tour resumed on stage 9 the next day.

Cadel only told five people about his injury—none of them riders—before the stage, to avoid denting his teammates' morale on his first day in the yellow jersey, which ended with him finishing 8 minutes and 9 seconds behind the stage winner, Sandy Casar of France. It was only when he stopped and, in tears, sank his head onto the shoulder of

Italian teammate Mauro Santambrogio that he first revealed the extent of his injury.

Most would have understood had he abandoned the Tour in 2010, but those who know him understand that simply wasn't an option for Cadel, who doesn't pull out of races unless his health is at risk.

His drive to finish in 2010 seemed fuelled by a sense of responsibility to Andy Rihs, the Swiss businessman who owns the team and BMC bike manufacturing firm—and to the new team he felt so much a part of. Cadel also wanted to honour the world champion's rainbow jersey he was wearing. But the challenge he faced in just reaching Paris after losing the yellow jersey was immense—especially after a career-worst time trial on stage 19 from Bordeaux to Paulliac.

Cadel went flat out in the 52-kilometre time trial and placed 166th out of the 170 survivors, at 10 minutes 57 seconds to Swiss stage winner Fabian Cancellara (Saxo Bank-SunGard). He rode the course in the morning as if he were preparing to win the time trial, but didn't have any strength for the race. When a rider is injured or not well in a road stage, they can hide, suffer longer and hang in; but in a time trial, that 5 per cent less capacity is 5 per cent in seconds. A 5 per cent time gap is a lot, and it all comes out in a time trial. You can't push harder in a time trial—you're already pushing to your maximum.

Cadel was in survival mode in those last days of the Tour, just focusing on getting to the finish. He'd taken the yellow jersey with a broken arm and pushed himself to continue, but never recovered after the crash. It was still five days from the finish, but Cadel's determination to finish the race was evident.

Cadel's reign in yellow only lasted that one day in the Alps, but for BMC it was still cause for celebration. Obviously they would have preferred to take the yellow jersey to Paris, but working together in such a difficult situation had brought the team together.

What was clear after the 2010 Tour was that Cadel and the BMC team shared a seriously strong faith in each other for another tilt at the Tour in 2011. The foundation of that faith was built during the year; but it was clear during the 2010 Tour that it was built with purpose—as it was after the Tour's finish, when the team feted the race at Le 1515. It seemed that Cadel had, at last, found a cycling family that suited him.

•   •   •

That Cadel finally achieved a Tour without bad luck in 2011 was due in no small part to the way he and his team raced and prepared for the event. He spent his downtime after the 2010 Tour going to the physio and orthopaedic surgeon every day, and then went to a training camp to prepare for the world championships.

Planning for the 2011 Tour de France continued as Cadel put in hours of preparation for the world championships under the guidance of his Italian trainer and mentor Aldo Sassi, who was fighting against the debilitating effects of a brain tumour. BMC needed to be stronger for the mountains, and its race program could be better tailored to another crack at the Tour if the team were awarded a first division ProTeam licence, which would allow it automatic entry into all world tour events and grand tours like the Tour.

Victory in the Tour de France may have been Cadel's ultimate objective, and the foundations of planning for the 2011 race may have begun, but the idea of winning it was still a long way from becoming a reality. The world titles were around the corner, but the really hard work was still to come ...

2

DEFENDING THE RAINBOW JERSEY

Disappointments in the 2010 Tour de France failed to dilute Cadel Evans' desire to finish the season on a high. As the defending world road champion, he still wanted to honour the rainbow jersey that he won at the championships in Mendrisio, Switzerland, the year before. And in no race did he wish to honour it more than in the 2010 world titles on the roads of Geelong, near his home town of Barwon Heads, Australia.

It was a race he wanted to prepare well for, and it was his focus as he recovered from the elbow fracture he sustained in the Tour. After finishing the Tour, the plan started with getting healthy, and then fit. That last week of racing wasn't as heavy as it might have been if BMC had been fighting to win it, but psychologically it was clearly fatiguing.

Cadel's elbow needed to heal before it could allow the extension required to ride on the road again. As an athlete, it is important to utilise each hour of each day to speed up the recovery process and to do whatever training the body will allow. While the rest of Europe was enjoying their summer holidays, Cadel worked with physiotherapist Luca Ruiz and Swiss orthopaedic surgeon Danilo Togninalli to ensure his elbow healed properly.

When he was ready for on-the-bike training, he went with Karsten Kroon, Alessandro Ballan and Mauro Santambrogio to the mountains in Livigno and trained. He did a couple of one-day races and then went and joined the national team.

For Cadel, accompanied also by his wife, Chiara, and dog, Molly, the trip to Livigno was perhaps as symbolic as it was practical. It was in Livigno that he had laid the foundations and fine-tuned his conditioning for his 2009 world title win. Returning to Livigno to train for the 2010 titles—with the rainbow jersey on his back—completed the cycle.

•   •   •

Cadel's eventual impact on the race belied the chances he had given himself beforehand, when he repeatedly played down his chances of winning, even though a number of insiders suspected he stood a far better chance than he was letting on.

Aldo Sassi's faith was so strong that, despite his rapidly deteriorating health, he flew from Italy to Australia to attend the titles. He was accompanied by his wife, Mariana, who is terrified of flying, but who travelled to look after Sassi. It was a big trip for someone in Sassi's state of health, and it was a strong show of confidence in Cadel. Cadel didn't talk with Sassi in Australia, but he had prepared as well as he could under a program devised by the Italian, and Sassi's presence could only have been a boost to his morale: a coach may often tell a rider that he can win, but when someone in such ill health puts their life at risk, it says a lot more.

Just how much Cadel felt for the 51-year-old Sassi was clear when he spoke to journalists before a final training ride on the 15.9-kilometre Geelong world title circuit. 'He has four untreatable tumours in the upper part of his brain. Just for him to make the trip out here was something', Cadel said. He continued on to say that were it not for the Italian, he probably would not have found the motivation to defend his title:

> First you've got to win it. But certainly the motivation—most people in my [situation] would have stopped their season after the Tour. I had a broken arm, and I was out. I want to fight it to the end while Aldo is still around with us and give it everything I've got, as he has given to my career since we've started working together.
>
> His situation has certainly pushed me a lot further than I would have otherwise gone this year. That's what got me through, actually, thinking of the difficulty he, and particularly his family, are going through.

Cadel revealed that, come the inevitable moments in the race when his legs start to burn, his lungs rasp and his heart races, he would tap into his thoughts about Sassi: 'If I'm suffering, it will be voluntary suffering, as opposed to [the] involuntary suffering he and his family are going through.'

But Sassi's determination in the face of poor health was not all that Cadel drew strength from. On his mind was his friend and former professional cyclist Paul Crake, who suffered spinal injuries in a bike crash in 2006:

Unfortunately, each year in the last few years [with] some close friend or relative, it's been the same thing. With the bushfires or whatever, every year you're there in the snow thinking: 'Oh God, I've got to go home. I should quit here, I should quit here.' Then you think, 'Oh no, there's someone here who's lost the use of his legs, Paul Crake, who would give anything to be here in my situation'. So I will keep going— that's got me through a lot.

There were many who believed that Cadel could win a second world title. So strong was the belief of the BMC soigneur Freddy Viaene, whose many tasks include ordering new clothing for the BMC team staff and riders, that he refused Cadel's request for a new BMC team racing kit to wear after the Worlds. Cadel, wanting to prepare for his races after the Worlds, had asked for the kit on the assumption he would not win, and as a result lose the privilege of wearing the world champion's jersey. But Viaene was not so sure Cadel wouldn't spend another year in the rainbow jersey, and delayed the order.

Though Cadel would have been be the first to admit that he had his sights set on a second world title, the attention the coveted rainbow jersey brings can be overwhelming. It is a great honour for any rider to wear the jersey in races and in training—in the cycling world, it is possibly the most distinguished marking possible. It is sometimes said to 'curse' a rider, perhaps a result of the attention the rainbow stripes bring.

The 2010 world titles course in Geelong wasn't one ideally suited to Cadel, even though seasoned observers still predicted he would leave a greater mark than he was suggesting he might—the reason being that, while the two short but steep climbs on the circuit were hard, the recovery time between them allowed the sprinters to come back into the race.

Cadel was not the only contender in the Australian team, which was allowed a full complement of nine riders because of the nation's world ranking. Also in the team were Baden Cooke, Allan Davis, Simon Gerrans, Matt Goss, Matt Hayman, Stuart O'Grady, Michael Rogers and Wes Sulzberger.

The race exploded after Ukraine's Oleksandr Kvachuk, the last survivor of a five-man breakaway that escaped early and got a maximum lead of more than 23 minutes, was caught on the first hill of lap nine by 31 riders—including Cadel, Gerrans and O'Grady—led by Italy's Vincenzo Nibali and Giovanni Visconti. Then a group of 12 riders, including Cadel, formed; it split and regrouped on lap 10 after a flurry of attacks. But they were caught by a diminishing peloton that included Australian Davis, whose hope of winning hinged on the race finishing in a small bunch sprint.

Belgian race favourite Philippe Gilbert attacked on the circuit's first hill to force a five-man breakaway that again included Cadel, who was certainly honouring his race number as the defending champion. However, the move was reeled in by the peloton with 4 or 5 kilometres to go, ensuring

Davis was in with a chance to win the world crown. Davis raced to a bronze medal in a sprint behind Norwegian Thor Hushovd, who took first place, and Dane Matti Breschel, who took second.

Even without the result Cadel wanted, being in Geelong with the No. 1 on his back was something special. The Australian team raced well before a cheering 10,000-strong home crowd in what was destined to be a once-in-a-lifetime opportunity for each of those who took part.

The Australian team wasn't spared criticism though—not for how it raced, but because it prepared at the Australian Institute of Sport in Canberra for all but the last day before the race, while foreign teams based themselves in Geelong and embraced the atmosphere that was building by the day.

Many felt the Australian team should have followed suit to adapt to the atmosphere and minimise the potential for the occasion to get to them on race day, and also to promote the event. The world titles were fighting for publicity with the Australian Football League grand final replay between Collingwood and St Kilda in Melbourne, and the National Rugby League grand final between the St George Illawarra Dragons and Sydney Roosters in Sydney—all of which were happening in the same week.

The Australian management defended its decision at the time, and many—including Cadel, who sets race planning and preparation as the top priority—still feel that staying in Canberra was the right thing to do.

Among the reasons given for the team's decision to remain in Canberra was concern over the possibility of bad weather in Geelong disrupting the pre-race training; and the team being able to avoid the distraction that so often comes with a large and enthusiastic media presence. In the lead-up to important races most riders are keen to spend as much time as possible training and recovering without the pressures of a demanding media—and training in Canberra provided that opportunity.

Cadel's world title ride set him up with a solid foundation of racing kilometres to end the season after having recovered from the broken elbow he sustained in the Tour. He had returned to a good level for the Worlds; but with a shaky build-up, staying consistent was not going to be easy. He raced the end of the season on empty, without any results. The season-ending Giro di Lombardia one-day classic in Italy is a hard and hilly race: the wear and tear of a tough season, the crammed preparation for the Worlds and the tough race he unleashed sapped his remaining reserves.

There was, however, a sense of confidence for what 2011 would bring ... Cadel was not done with the Tour.

3

PLANNING AND RECRUITMENT FOR 2011

In October 2010 Cadel Evans sat down with his BMC team management. The world road championships in Geelong had come and gone, with the title passing from Cadel to Norway's Thor Hushovd. There was no time for regret. It was time to plan for the 2011 Tour de France.

BMC team president Jim Ochowicz and sports director John Lelangue set about putting in a system to help Cadel win the race, focusing on recruiting more climbers for support in the mountains. It was also widely suspected that the 2011 Tour would include a team time trial. BMC was already well into its preparation for a team time trial, with its continued development of a new time-trial bike that had begun a year earlier.

One of the first decisions Cadel made with Ochowicz, Lelangue, Aldo Sassi and Sassi's assistant, Andrea Morelli, was to devise a competition schedule for himself of about 30 to 33 days' racing before the Tour began on 2 July, compared to the 40 to 45 in 2010 and 45 in 2009.

But just as important was to develop a roster that would enable Cadel to be as effective as possible in the crucial stages of the Tour. As committed and willing as his team-mates had shown themselves to be in the 2010 Tour, it was clear he needed more help in the mountains.

This was understandable considering Cadel's late arrival to BMC. Before he had even put pen to paper with BMC, all of the riders on the team had been signed—and, except for George Hincapie, none had any idea of his imminent arrival. The deal was still being discussed when the team met in late October 2009 for their annual planning meeting for the season ahead. It was not until they convened for a training camp soon after that they were told that 'a new recruit' would be joining them; they were stunned after learning during the announcement that it would be Cadel. However, once he'd signed on, Cadel and BMC had known that they would have to manage with the roster they had for 2010.

• • •

BMC sports director John Lelangue first met Cadel just after the 2009 world titles when he, Andy Rihs, Jim Ochowicz and George Hincapie took the Australian rider and his wife, Chiara, for dinner to talk about a possible program. But he had been observing Cadel's career for a while and admired his tenacity:

> He was always so close. He was always there, fighting in the time trial, fighting in the mountains, a complete rider … really good in detail and preparation. He was also English-speaking, which was important for us as an American team. So integration into the team was not a problem. I was confident that he was the right guy in the right place, even

if some people were saying he is always the guy who places
second or third, or that he is too old, or will never win ...
I really believed that we could go for it with him in the
stage races.

·At dinner that night Lelangue felt that Cadel would fit
with BMC. What began as a social dinner at the Al Porto
hotel became a detailed planning meeting that went late
into the night, and resumed at breakfast early the next day:

I had my ideas and Cadel had his ideas. From there he left
and then ... when he was in Australia for a long period, we
made an agreement to phone each other every three days
to keep talking about everything. And then we met 10 days
before the Tour Down Under.

That Cadel was the world champion gave the BMC team
a massive boost in purpose and self-esteem, and gave it the
confidence to tackle a year in which its Tour entry hinged on
it proving its worth as a wildcard entry. Hence, the team—led
by Cadel—attacked the early season aggressively. In January
in the Tour Down Under, where Cadel first met his new
teammates and placed sixth overall, he, Alejandro Valverde,
Luis León Sánchez and Peter Sagan starred in a headlining
attack on the second of two ascents of Old Willunga Hill,
which became an all-time race highlight.

And from there BMC continued to impress with results,
without even knowing its 2010 Tour fate. Cadel took third
place in the Tirreno–Adriatico stage race in Italy, first in the

Flèche-Wallonne one-day classic in Belgium, fifth in Liège–Bastogne–Liège, and a stage 7 win and fifth place overall in the Giro d'Italia, in which he also won the points competition and placed fourth in the mountains category—despite falling ill early on. Lelangue says:

> Having the world champion on your team is good for the riders, for the sports directors … it's a kind of honour. You can be proud of it but also it's a responsibility. You know that it's only for one year and that you have a certain value to represent.

Lelangue was impressed with how Cadel embraced the uncertainty of their Tour invitation:

> We could have said 'no' to the Giro and preserved our leader for the Tour without knowing until April if we were going … and if we didn't, [we] could have ended up not taking a rider like Cadel to a grand tour that year, which wouldn't have been good for him or the team—he was the world champion. But we took the risk and said 'yes' to the Giro. Then a couple of weeks before the Giro we received confirmation about the Tour. It would not have been honest to say to the Giro organiser, 'Now that we are going to the Tour we don't need to send Cadel or a strong team [to the Giro]'. So we did it.

It still amazes Lelangue that, when Cadel fell ill the day after his stage win at Montalcino in horribly wet conditions, he summoned the strength of mind and body to continue and finish so well. The 8th stage was the longest of the Giro, at 265 kilometres. Cadel had a temperature of 39 degrees Celsius and his fever had kept him awake all night:

> He was really sick. He didn't come to dinner and I went to his room to see him, and again in the morning I went to his room … he was really, really bad. I was sure that he would quit the stage because of this. I'm sure that if you put an average rider who was in the same physical condition as he was on that day, that 99 per cent of them would quit. That was the worst stage to be really sick … There was a big group of 40 riders going, and we didn't chase them because we didn't want to communicate to anyone that he was sick. I wasn't sure [that] if he asked the guys, 'Let's close the gap', that he would not be dropped. I said, 'Keep it quiet'. We lost a lot of time, but his form came back and he finished fifth.

Whatever was to happen in the 2010 Tour de France after such a strong start with BMC, the faith and belief of the team in Cadel—and he in the team—had been forged. It strengthened when Cadel backed up from the Giro in the Tour; after a terrific ride over the cobblestones of stage 3 he took the race leader's yellow jersey on stage 8 to Morzine-Avoriaz in the Alps—and in doing so accrued an overall lead of 1 minute and 1 second on the defending champion, Alberto Contador. Unfortunately, it was also on stage 8 that Cadel crashed and fractured his left elbow, only to lose the Tour lead on stage 9 and struggle to the finish in Paris.

As disappointing as Cadel's fate must have been for Cadel, BMC regarded one Tour start, one day in the yellow jersey, a heroic finish by its new world champion leader—and the buoyant spirit throughout the team—as a huge success. As Lelangue says:

> I was really happy because we went to the end. It was a victory. We did it. We were at the Tour to the finish and with the world champion. There was a lot of criticism when we took Cadel—from journalists, former riders and in France—that we had taken the place of another French team in the Tour. They said we have Cadel, but nobody else. At least we proved that we were there with a strong team, that we could go for it, we could compete. That was a victory and I told Cadel that. And we proved that we could take the yellow jersey.

Cadel's immediate goal after the Tour was to recover and rebuild for the end-of-season races—his last in the world champion's jersey.

He was unable to fulfil the program he had planned, but still impressed his increasing legion of fans in the races he did compete in—smaller events like the Kampioenschap van Vlaanderen in Koolskamp, Belgium, in September, which was won by Australian Leigh Howard. Cadel was feted for simply starting. Because of his elbow injury, the race organiser had assumed he would not be able to race. Lelangue recalls how he took the news that Cadel would in fact race: 'He said, "Wow". It was such a party, and there we were attacking. Cadel was not there just for training.' From

Koolskamp, Cadel raced in the Grand Prix des Fourmies in northern France where, Lelangue says, 'There were so many people from this city because there the race is like Christmas. And all the old people came to me and said, "Thank you for bringing the world champion"'.

• • •

2010 was anything but a failure for Cadel and BMC. The team was only in the Tour after having been granted a wildcard, but it experienced the high of racing in the yellow jersey—albeit for only one day. The season had been challenging, and at times distressing; but that they all reached the end realising how well they fared was reason to cheer.

Cadel had an inkling of this before the Tour finished in Paris, telling journalists in Paulliac after that last time trial:

We have experienced a spectrum of outcomes that can happen on the Tour. That can only serve us for the future. If we look back on November or December of last year, [the idea of] BMC with the yellow jersey at the Tour … I don't think anyone would have taken to that well. But [team co-owner and president] Jim Ochowicz had a vision. It's still a work in process, but it's one step in that process.

It's not just about this year and building up a team for this year's Tour, or the Tour in 2012 or whenever. It takes a long time. Every step of the way we learn something, we improve things—especially this year. It's been a real learning experience. We have been close for stage wins and we've had the yellow jersey taken off to get X-rays as well.

Cadel may not have had the Tour result he had planned for, but his calmness and the attacking flair he had shown throughout the year in honour of his world champion's rainbow jersey said enough. It was a season that included a win in the Flèche-Wallonne one-day classic in Belgium, fifth place overall and a stage win in the Giro d'Italia, and a world No. 1 ranking. He had also earned his teammates' trust and their commitment to put their all into his Tour campaign. And he'd enjoyed it:

> It's been really enjoyable to be with them, despite the lack of results. Outside of taking the results away, it's been a really enjoyable Tour. I've had a good group of people around us. An optimistic attitude is the biggest change of environment I'm in now. That goes a long way, especially when things aren't going well. When you think why the hell you're doing it, a little bit of optimism goes a long way.

By the end of Cadel's first year in the BMC team, it seemed clear what BMC needed to do to be successful in the 2011 Tour. The Andy and Fränk Schleck combination was still going to be a hard one to go against. No other team had two such exceptionally strong climbers.

But by the time Cadel had recovered and closed the year with an impressive ride in the world titles in Geelong, BMC team management had already set about bolstering the ranks.

A lot of strategy and timing goes into the process of recruiting experienced riders earmarked for performance in the Tour. Throughout the season the rumour mill spins madly about riders who are purported to be in talks with new teams, although under a Union Cycliste Internationale (UCI) rule, no team may court a rider from another team before 1 August.

To plan a big acquisition and build a real team takes more than the weeks and months that are often spoken about in the press. To get a group of high-quality riders together takes years. To build a winning team in the second year, as BMC had, was already huge progress. But to recruit a big name in the sport, you've got to start talking to them well before their contract runs out.

One of BMC's principal recruits was Italian Ivan Santaromita, who lives near Cadel and his wife, Chiara, in Stabio, and is also trained by Andrea Morelli. Other important additions included Italian Manuel Quinziato, whose strength and time-trialling prowess was highly valued, and Frenchman Amaël Moinard, a rider whose decision to switch to a foreign team came as a surprise to some. Of course, BMC recruited elsewhere, with the Swiss Johann Tschopp, and American Taylor Phinney and Australian Tim Roe joining from the Livestrong-Trek team—but they were all recruited with a view to the future, and not considered part of BMC's grand plan for the 2011 Tour.

At BMC it is team president Jim Ochowicz who ultimately makes recruiting decisions, though he also seeks feedback from a couple of riders—the leaders, such as Cadel—and some of the sports directors.

A potential recruit's qualities as a bike rider are the main considerations, but—as with teams of any sort—having a personality that syncs with the 'team personality' is often just as important. There is no need for big team-building and motivational exercises or projects if the right people are chosen initially. Everyone wants to do their job and do their best for the team, whether they're signed to be a team leader, or if they're there for the team time trial or the Giro or the Tour or the classics.

All rookies who join BMC are given time to adapt to the demands of top-tier professional racing, no matter their record. Of course they are expected to work hard and be professional and learn and improve, but they are not pressured to produce results right away—a rider who's self-motivated doesn't need extra pressure. If the right rider has been selected, and they're provided with good teammates, good equipment and a realistic race program, there's no need to push them.

• • •

BMC's rider recruitment was in place, and Cadel had to focus on his preparation for the 2011 Tour—from a training and race schedule to course stage reconnaissance.

Omitted from his race plan for the year was the Tour Down Under in Adelaide—the January world tour opener that he raced in 2010, his first with BMC. Instead, the 2011 racing year for him was to begin in March with the Giro del Friuli and Montepaschi Strade Bianche, lower-key one-day events, and then the Tirreno–Adriatico stage race, followed by the Flèche-Wallonne mid-week classic in the Belgian Ardennes and—pending form—possibly Liège–Bastogne–Liège in April. This was followed by the Tour de Romandie in Switzerland, Critérium du Dauphiné in France, and several training camps to prepare for the Tour's mountain stages and the team time trial.

Cadel's 2011 race schedule was decided in late October at a BMC team and staff planning meeting in Legano, near Castellanza and the Mapei Training Centre created by Aldo Sassi. The team meeting was held after the Giro di Lombardia, the team's last major race of the year, and just before the 2011 Tour route presentation in Paris.

A world tour team has about 400 race days they are obliged to race, and only 28 or 30 riders to fill them; it's not like there are 28 or 30 riders that are always fit and healthy and ready to race from January to October filling in the gaps behind Cadel. Each rider in the team needs a fair and reasonable program.

The Tour is of central importance to the BMC team, and so the 12 or 15 riders who might be on the Tour generally get priority on their race programs to build towards July. After that it's a bit of juggling: everyone has their day and all the race positions are filled, but people get sick or injured, so there needs to be some flexibility.

The importance of the Tour also affects 'the plan', hence the anticipation that mounts in the lead-up to the annual presentation of the next year's route. Before the Tour is announced, most teams know what areas they need to improve and, thanks to the rumour mill that surrounds cycling, have some idea of what the route will entail: before the course is unveiled, a number of its characteristics have usually already been announced—or even leaked. The Tour presentation is just the final confirmation.

The 2011 Tour route presentation confirmed for BMC that it needed to have a good team time trial, and allowed Cadel and the team management to devise a race strategy that placed him in the best possible position to secure victory in the Tour.

However, the blueprint was not locked in for good until after Cadel had liaised with Sassi, and Andrea Morelli, who became Cadel's principal trainer following Sassi's passing in December 2010. Planning for the year ahead was meticulous and carried out in meetings at Sassi's house before he died and at the Mapei Training Centre Sassi ran in nearby Castellanza.

The result was a careful combination of racing, training and recovery periods, altitude training camps and course reconnaissance. At Cadel's age, he was best able to use the base of training and racing he already had in his legs if he had time to recover. The overall plan was a big change from what Cadel had done before and allowed him to focus on the quality, rather than the quantity, of the races in his program.

•   •   •

As much as Cadel's career-defining 2011 Tour win was a result of his ability and self-belief, and the faith and planning of Sassi, it was also reflective of the faith of his team-mates; his team sponsor, BMC, and the vision of its owner, Andy Rihs; and Cadel's European agent, the former Swiss Giro d'Italia winner and Tour contender Tony Rominger, who sealed the deal for him to join the BMC team after the 2009 season.

Rominger's idea when he steered Cadel to his eventual signing with the BMC team was that, with a rider like Cadel, BMC could go to the Tour, see how they performed, and then start slowly to build a team around him. No-one could have foreseen that within two years they'd already have won the Tour.

Cadel is no longer a rider whose career as a Tour contender is at the crossroads, as many observers had considered it was back then. He is now a Tour champion. Amazingly, it all fell into place at BMC far earlier than anyone anticipated.

To observers it's clear that one of the biggest factors in that success was that BMC had faith in Cadel, which was really all he needed. He can race a bike. He knows what he needs to do to win the big races. If you allow him to do that, and take a rest and skip the smaller races that would probably compromise his performance at bigger ones—then, with a good team, deliver him to the final of the big hard races—he can finish the job. Which is exactly what BMC discovered ...

4

REBUILDING BODY, MIND, BIKE AND TEAM

By the time Cadel Evans had returned to Switzerland, in time for Christmas, his long-time trainer and mentor Aldo Sassi had died—he passed away on 12 December 2010. When Cadel made it back to his European home, he was set to train in the solitude of a European winter for the very first time, which allowed him, firstly, to escape the distractions that come with training back in Australia; and secondly, to do so knowing that he was near the home of Sassi who, in his absence, still had an impact on Cadel's training.

The suffering that Sassi had experienced throughout his fight with cancer could only have hardened Cadel's resolve to go that little bit further when he was struggling—or when the going got tough, such as when there was poor weather outside.

As an Australian, Cadel hadn't seen a full winter since 1994, and even then he took time out of it to travel to Cairns in Far North Queensland to race. It was all new; there weren't enough daylight hours above freezing to finish off a long ride outdoors, so he had to add extra time with a session on the rollers indoors. It was a big change for him, but psychologically it was beneficial: it was very quiet and he was able to spend quality time with Chiara and to train uninterrupted.

Because Cadel knew he might not be able to train some

days due to winter weather conditions, and because his mother and her partner, Geoff, were going to spend the Christmas period with him and Chiara, he began riding earlier than he would have were he in Australia, where he could ride through the summer. Furthermore, because Cadel had ruled out racing in the Tour Down Under in January, there was less need for him to be in strong form so early on.

When an elite cyclist takes a month off and then gets back on the bike, they are comparatively unfit. And when a rider's racing program spans the entire season—as Cadel's typically has—they are expected to be in top form very quickly. A rushed build-up can lead to hit-and-miss results. In 2011 Cadel had two months to get ready slowly and build up a good, solid base, which brought him to excellent form in a more sustainable way.

Cadel had resumed cycling in Australia in mid-November from his home in Barwon Heads, with short rides that focused on him turning the legs over rather than riding hard.

As he didn't have to ramp up too quickly, he worked on regaining his base level of fitness, and then on his strength and endurance. Riders with years of experience know how much is just enough and how much is too much, and try to work within those parameters. It can be challenging to juggle training with travel and other professional commitments, and requires a great deal of time management.

In the time Cadel has called Barwon Heads home, his profile as a cyclist has risen, and that's part of being accepted there. But his increasing popularity sometimes became a hurdle. Often, he would find himself joined by local cyclists wanting to ride with him—and in many cases try and beat him—on his training rides.

Cadel's gym program in the 2010–2011 off-season began under the eye of former Geelong AFL club trainer Paul Haines, overseen by another local physiotherapist Konrad Slavinskis; and then, when he returned to Switzerland, continued with his Italian physiotherapist and osteopath Luca Ruiz, who helped Cadel to develop his core stability and efficiency on the bike.

Cadel's association with the Geelong Football Club began in 2008 when he was recovering from a knee injury sustained in a post–Tour de France party that compromised his participation in the Olympic Games at Beijing. The football club has a great deal of experience with knee injuries, and offered to help with his rehabilitation.

The media often focuses on the scandals surrounding footballers, but in getting to know the club, Cadel saw how the players train, and how dedicated and professional they are. It was a unique opportunity to gain insight into the training methods used at the elite level of a sport other than cycling.

In late January Cadel joined his BMC teammates for a training camp at Denia, south of Valencia in Spain. It was the hardest he'd ridden that season, and he was far from the level he would need to be at in July, but it was clear he was on the right path. With experience, athletes learn to channel their time and energy as efficiently as possible. For riders like Cadel, it is work in the gym and slow kilometres on the road in the early season that produce a solid base of strength and endurance.

WHERE THE GRASS IS NOW ALWAYS GREENER ...

Ever since 1914, when Victorians Snowy Munro and Don Kirkham became the first Australians to compete in the Tour de France, people have dreamed of an Australian winning the race. But as the sport has continued to blossom in Australia, with interest and participation in elite and amateur competition increasing by the year, people have dreamed of an Australian team racing the Tour—and, as of 2012, that dream is set to be a reality.

In December 2011 the Union Cycliste Internationale confirmed that the Australian Orica-GreenEDGE team had been granted a first division ProTeam licence for two years, ensuring entry to all world tour events and the three grand tours: the Tour de France, Giro d'Italia and Vuelta a España.

The 30-rider team is backed by Melbourne businessman Gerry Ryan, owner of Jayco caravans; Mitchelton Wines; a number of racehorses, including the 2010 Melbourne Cup winner Americain; and Global Creatures, the production company behind the world-acclaimed animatronic show *Walking with Dinosaurs*.

Before Orica-GreenEDGE's ProTeam status was confirmed, many felt that the team would need an Australian Tour contender, and who better than Cadel Evans?

Cadel had held behind-the-scenes talks with various parties in Australia about the possible creation of an Australian team. But by the time Orica-GreenEDGE was launched, he was already signed and committed to BMC—and he felt the American team's ambitions, program and resources were better suited to his career needs.

Cadel's moral support for Orica-GreenEDGE never wavered though. With the approval of his BMC team, Cadel attended a Orica-GreenEDGE press conference on 28 May 2011 at the Australian Institute of Sport's new European Training Centre in Varese, Italy—not far from his home in Stabio, Switzerland.

Cadel's support for Orica-GreenEDGE was nothing to do with any secret deals or hedging of bets with BMC; it was a genuine belief in the benefits of what having a team like Orica-GreenEDGE could be for world and Australian cycling, and those behind it.

What is least understood in a lot of international analysis of the Orica-GreenEDGE project, and those who are behind it, is that its main benefactor—Gerry Ryan—is not a fly-by-night supporter of Australian cycling; his support of the creation of an Australian team is not driven by self-interest. While he has also sponsored the Melbourne Storm National Rugby League team and St Kilda Australian Football League side, Ryan has been one of the longest serving financial backers of Australian cycling and

of many low-profile athletes and sports.

Cadel, who has known Ryan since his early mountain biking days, has also supported Orica-GreenEDGE because of another key figure behind it—former Cycling Australia high performance director Shayne Bannan, who is the team's general manager and the one who convinced Ryan to get behind the initiative. Cadel has said that Bannan is the only person in Australia he had complete faith could bring an Australian team to the Tour. He's a man of few words, but they are normally ones that, when said, are worth listening to.

However, as positive as the arrival of Orica-GreenEDGE to the peloton is, it would not be the team for Cadel: Orica-GreenEDGE began as a team for one-day races and stage wins, which suits the majority of Australian professionals, but not Cadel. It also came too late. Perhaps if it had come after the 2009 Tour it would have been a different story, but Cadel had already made a substantial commitment to a team that believed in him.

And at the launch of the European Training Centre, Cadel confirmed that he would most probably ride out the rest of his career with BMC, telling journalists:

We have built up something—we have worked a lot to get to where we are now. I want to continue with that. I'm committed, not signed, but committed with BMC for life. BMC came to me in 2009 when about five people in the world of cycling seemed to have faith in me ...

Cadel has since reached new heights with BMC—on so many levels, it is a team very well suited to him, and he is a rider well suited to BMC.

• • •

Critical to any Tour campaign is the research and technology that goes behind equipment—especially for the most important tool of the trade, the bicycle. With BMC being a Swiss bicycle manufacturer, obviously no stone was left unturned in this area.

The net result of two years of research, development and testing in the wind tunnel and on the track by BMC's team of engineers and designers was the time-trial bike that Cadel would ride to victory in the 2011 Tour. Finding time to test equipment is a big challenge for any team, considering the program of races and essential training camps. But it is important that testing is carried out properly; for BMC, the best opportunity came in a scheduled one-week break after the Tour de Romandie in May.

The location of the wind tunnel BMC used in 2011 is confidential at the facility's request, although it is in Europe.

Ideally testing would be done in January, but equipment needs to be approved by the UCI—and sometimes the regulations for position can change mid-season. The equipment needs to be tested, but there also needs to be time to develop it or adapt it to a new position: building a bike can take several years.

Cadel's personal mechanic, Antonio Biron, did not play a role in the development of Cadel's bikes, although his role afterwards was absolutely imperative. Biron lives near Cadel, and, as most of the reliability testing and adaption is done in training, his addition to the BMC staff line-up made a huge difference.

Those who worked closest on testing with the engineers and designers were Andrea Morelli, a biomechanist and now Cadel's trainer, and Stefano Cattai, the Italian former professional cyclist who now liaises between the BMC manufacturer and the team to provide the feedback from testing.

Morelli has a unique set of qualifications, and his research and experience are practical and balanced. Obviously his expertise is useful for Cadel's performance, but his involvement in the testing is also utilised in the design of the BMC team's equipment. It's almost unique in the cycling industry: a close working relationship between designers, manufacturers, and a biomechanist who actually is also a trainer.

Cattai's main job is to represent the riders' needs to the engineers and designers, and getting those ideas into products to be used in the races. Having a bicycle manufacturer as the main team sponsor facilitates that happening.

Wind-tunnel testing is a laborious process that takes time and patience, because of the extensive collation of data and the need to repeat tests to confirm and validate results. Furthermore, for the most part, wind-tunnel testing requires the rider to stay in one set position, rather than actually pedal as if they are on the road or track. The limitation is that the measurements only give an indication of performance in a headwind, with a static rider—changes in wind speed and direction, changes in rider position, and the turbulence produced by the rider are not accounted for, and all of these factors can change the results dramatically.

Hence, while wind-tunnel testing is more for equipment than position, the importance for Cadel of having a biomechanist attend can't be overstated. The key factors assessed are the biomechanical, physiological and aerodynamic optimal positions, which are all put into practical use while riding on a velodrome.

The velodrome used by BMC is at Montichiari, a covered 250-metre track made of Siberian pine at a cost of €15 million. It was opened in May 2009—the first of its kind in Italy—and built to bring Italian riders to their peak for the 2012 Olympic Games, as well as for use by other athletes, like Cadel.

Unlike testing in a wind tunnel, where riders must remain stationary, in velodrome testing riders can ride their bikes.

It's not all done at full speed—there are a lot of pauses in the riding to change the equipment combinations. It is a long and often tedious process, but exhaustive testing can result in a rider winning seconds per kilometre.

5

ROAD TO THE VENDÉE AND THE TOUR START

Despite all the planning for 2011, Cadel Evans began the racing year earlier than intended—on 3 March with the Giro del Friuli, where his wife, Chiara, studied classical piano many years before, and where the two had taken time out for a small holiday after a disappointing Tour de France in 2009. The Giro del Friuli was followed on 5 March by the Montepaschi Strade Bianche race on the dirt roads of southern Tuscany, where he won a stage of the 2010 Giro d'Italia.

In racing the Giro del Friuli, Cadel was able to get some racing kilometres in before the more intense Strade Bianche. It poured rain; the group Cadel was in stopped because of the bad weather, and he didn't finish. Cadel's form progressed in Tuscany, although he was a long way behind his ex-teammate and the day's winner Philippe Gilbert. Nevertheless, at the end of the race—which many professionals ride just because they like it so much—he had some early-season race kilometres in his legs.

There was more reasoning behind the decision to start racing earlier than originally planned. With a number of riders coming from the Tour Down Under in Adelaide and the tours of Qatar and Oman to start in the Tirreno–

Adriatico from 9 to 15 March, it seemed the field would be at a higher level of condition than in previous years.

Cadel's decision to bring forward his season start paid handsome dividends: by stage 5 of Tirreno, supported by his teammates—especially the seasoned George Hincapie and Alessandro Ballan—he was in the race leader's blue jersey. He had been too far back; Hincapie's experienced eye had seen that Cadel needed to be more in front and encouraged him to do that stage hard. He got Cadel in front, and the BMC team was all hands on deck for the win. The race split, Robert Gesink was dropped, and Cadel took the leader's jersey.

Hincapie today looks back on Cadel's response as a turning point in the way his teammates regarded him:

> He could rely a lot more on the team and most were strong—
> we also knew we didn't have all of our Tour team there—and
> that probably gave him motivation. All of a sudden, I felt I
> started to see him feeling really good, and I was enthusiastic,
> motivated and I was having fun again … so I was starting to
> really look forward to the Tour.

Cadel has always been drawn to the Tirreno–Adriatico, because of his familiarity with the Italian roads, the atmosphere of the race and the suitability of the course's specific design. He had wanted to race the Tirreno in previous years, but the classics riders always had priority in the teams he rode with.

Although Cadel has always been based in Switzerland, Italy is the culture with which he is most familiar and comfortable in Europe, and he makes no secret of the fact that he feels more comfortable racing in Italy—which, after Switzerland, is virtually his second home-country.

His attachment to Italy dates from his first visit to Europe in 1995 for the junior road Worlds; it grew through racing with Shayne Bannan and the Australian Under-23 team, starting out as a road pro with Saeco–Cannondale, working at Mapei with Aldo Sassi, and meeting his wife, Chiara. Cadel now has family and a wealth of friends and colleagues in Italy, and has done most of his racing there.

Cadel is suited to the racing style of the Tirreno–Adriatico. Generally the climbs are a bit shorter than those in Paris–Nice; there are more classics riders and so the emphasis is more on getting position for the climbs rather than hitting them and going full-out for five or 10 minutes against pure climbers. Some observers felt that the course's array of steep but shorter climbs helped Cadel to develop his attacking punch.

The one hiccup for Cadel in his 2011 roster was when he was forced to reduce the number of race days by three after injuring his vastus medialis—the muscle above the knee, part of the quadriceps group—while mountain biking near his home at Stabio, Switzerland. As a precaution, Cadel missed the two Belgian Ardennes classics—Flèche-Wallonne, which he won in 2010, and Liège–Bastogne–Liège, which he was to race pending his form at Flèche-Wallonne; and the Amstel Gold Race in the Netherlands. He underwent rehabilitation with a view to returning for the Tour de Romandie from 26 April to 1 May.

Cadel sustained the injury when he hit his knee on the top tube of his mountain bike in a crash while cross-training.

He was exploring a trail and discovered—a bit too late—that it was a little too steep. The bruised bone and muscle above his knee swelled quickly and impressively, and he had to be picked up. When he got home he immediately called his local physiotherapist, Luca Ruiz, and the BMC team doctor, Max Testa, to get an initial diagnosis before alerting sports director John Lelangue to the mishap.

While Lelangue was disappointed, he was also reassuring about it. Being scratched from the Ardennes did have some benefits: it provided an opportunity for teammate Greg Van Avermaet to lead the team, and it allowed Cadel to save his resources for later. The Ardennes classics take a lot of time in training and preparation to race properly, and there's always the chance it could compromise a rider's performance in the Tour.

Because of the bruising on his femur, just above the knee, Cadel recovered only at the very last hour for the Tour de Romandie, though there was still speculation over his fitness. Sometimes the attention an athlete attracts when things are not going well can prove stressful, and can even compromise recovery and rehabilitation, but time was on Cadel's side. Trainer Andrea Morelli had him on a strict rehabilitation program that consisted of physiotherapy, ultrasound treatment and regular icing to enhance healing.

While a rider's body is able to rest a little in a period of injury, going to the physio or hospital two to three times a day and doing relatively mundane exercises can be quite tough mentally. Cadel still recovered well enough to line up for the Tour de Romandie start. He began the race touting realistic ambition, even though the race is the biggest of the year for his Swiss-sponsored team, after the Tour de France. He wasn't pessimistic about it, though; he was training well. He loved Romandy when he first moved to Europe, and knows most of the roads. Still, he arrived a day early to check the mountain-top finish with Lelangue, and once the race started his form and condition improved with every day of the tour. He rode well in the time trial and then took the lead.

Cadel's overall victory as a GC rider in the Tour de Romandie came with his eighth place at 45 seconds to American David Zabriskie (Garmin-Cervélo) in the stage 4 time trial over 20 kilometres from Aubonne to Signal de Bougy. Cadel's victory carried added gloss, coming as it did after he had just recovered from an injury. It meant that he was back on track. It also helped to reinforce his stature within the BMC team as a rider who could really be relied on to not just win, but to do so even when challenged by misfortune. He told the French newspaper *L'Equipe:*

I haven't given up on winning the Tour. I still believe in it, but perhaps the rest of the world doesn't. I just need a little bit of luck that was missing in 2008 and last year.

IN THE F1 FAST LANE

Two days before Cadel's final Tour lead-up race, the Critérium du Dauphiné in France (5 to 12 June), the long-list of riders in contention for a place on the BMC Tour team assembled at the Formula 1 race circuit in Zolder, Belgium. The purpose? A team time trial training camp. The venue was ideal, with a fast surface that included some challenging sweeping bends; but it was chosen primarily because it was a secure zone and free from the danger of unpredictable public traffic.

The course was also cost effective. BMC did not need to pay for fire and medical emergency services that are required for race cars, and they had all the specialist time-trial bikes they would use in the Tour already produced, assembled and set up. Usually it is a company's marketing department that decides when and how new products will be launched, but BMC was on a performance program, so the team started with a low-key training camp—not ideal for marketing, but perfect for preparing for the Tour.

The riders who attended the camp with Cadel were George Hincapie, Marcus Burghardt, Brent Bookwalter, Ivan Santaromita, Manuel Quinziato, Michael Schär, Steve Morabito, Amaël Moinard, Greg Van Avermaet and Taylor Phinney. The turnout and the conviction of every one of the BMC riders who took part was impressive, especially Van Avermaet, who knew he would not be racing in the Tour and was not obliged to attend.

The morning session at the camp gave the BMC riders an opportunity to organise their planned formation for the Tour's team time trial. Getting the right combination—where each rider knows after whom he will take the front position in the race, and for how long they will set tempo up front before dropping back to take last position in the formation—is absolutely vital for the best performance. And after their fourth place at the Tirreno–Adriatico in March, in which some felt BMC could have fared better, the visit to Zolder was extremely important.

The team time trial really is a team event: one team member's error has consequences for everyone. And in a race, one mistake quickly causes another mistake. Because of the dispersed nature of the professional cycling world, it is hard to bring together a team and really practise cooperating together as a soccer or football team would.

By the time the team time-trial squad convened, most of the BMC riders in the Tour long-list were already switching to Tour mode, says Hincapie:

In May already you're thinking every race is slowly getting you ready for the Tour, and then we do the team time-trial camp in early June.

It was a real pain in the ass to get to for a lot of us. I did the national championships in the US. The next morning I flew to Europe. I hadn't seen my family in a while so it was tough, but it was well worth it because we shocked everybody in the team time trial in the Tour. At our camp we did the work and there wasn't really anybody complaining about being there. They knew why we were there. You even saw guys there who knew they had little chance of going to the Tour, but they still wanted to be part of the preparation and were thinking, 'If something goes wrong, I want to be there, ready for it'. The management did really well in choosing the right personalities.

It was also important in that camp, says Hincapie, that everyone understood the intricacies of time-trialling and what made up the optimal formation. He says:

Cadel wanted to ride behind me, I'm pretty sure he was behind me in the end. Lance Armstrong always rode behind me … Maybe it was just that they trust my handling a bit more. I also call out little errors—guys coming back into the line too much, accelerating too much when they come to the front, or slowing down too much. I can see and call right away, especially in training. In training it's good to get the rhythm and feel of high speed from time trial, but a race is totally different. In training you're always at 90 per cent whereas in a race we're going at 100 per cent.

The most dangerous moment for a rider in a team time trial is when they drop off the front, slow down and then re-join the speeding line-up at its end. It's tough because they have to jump back in at speed. Obviously pulling at the front is also hard.

However, by the end of the camp and after the Tirreno–Adriatico

result, Hincapie was confident that BMC would pass muster in the Tour:

We knew we had the guys that could be up there for a good result … some of the best flat riders in the world. It was never really our specialty as far as those guys racing together, but we had done the work and we knew that if nothing went wrong, we'd be there up close.

While Cadel's past Tours had been cruelled by misfortune in the team time trial, Hincapie emphasised that preparation would minimise the chances of it happening again:

That's why we knew, when we did the team time-trial camps, how important it was. But if you look at the teams that Contador had there, and some of the other overall favourites, we thought we'd really try and get some time on them.

53

Cadel's win in the Tour de Romandie certainly was an enormous morale boost that came just at the right time, and it set the pace for Cadel and his team in the lead-up to his next and final event before the Tour: the Critérium du Dauphiné stage race in France. Knowing that his team was right behind him at such a crucial phase of his Tour preparation also reassured him. As he looked ahead to the Critérium du Dauphiné, he told the *Sydney Morning Herald* that his wins in Tirreno–Adriatico and Tour de Romandie.

… have been a little bit better than I expected for the year, which is always a good thing in terms of gaining confidence of the team. Not that I ever felt they lacked confidence in me, but it was good at the Tour de Romandie to go through the motions of having the [leader's] jersey. It's always a good role to go through and for everyone to be a part of looking towards the Tour.

This year the team has strengthened a little better in most areas, and that is always good for my part. I have [also] come in a lot fresher. This time last year, I [had just finished] the Giro [d'Italia]. And I had been sick during it and was pretty exhausted. This year, I come in with a lot more consistent build-up, and I am certainly feeling a fair bit fresher at this stage.

As well as a mid-January team training camp at Denia, Spain, and the team time-trial get-together, Cadel put himself through his paces at two high-altitude camps before the Tour—the most gruelling and challenging being in the

Pyrenees just before the BMC team assembled for the team time-trial camp. With him there was a small group including Santaromita, mechanic Ronald Ruyen, and friend and osteopath David Bombeke.

There are several reasons Cadel is cautious about revealing much about his high-altitude camps—their location, duration and number. Training camps are an opportunity for riders to focus on training without any of the distractions that come with the media and commitments to sponsors. Racing a Tour de France is a stressful process, and vital moments of downtime between rides are few and far between if you are in the results.

Riders occasionally come across some of their competitors out training in the mountains. Seeing their colleagues out riding is a social moment that many make the most of, but there are often members of the media in hot pursuit.

In the build-up to the Tour, media interest has grown for the reconnaissance trips the various teams make to important sections of the Tour. Riders make trips to check some of the climbs in the Pyrenees and the Alps, mostly to get an idea of the difficulty of the climbs and any dangers in the descents. These trips also offer the opportunity to enjoy the fantastic views and scenery that they miss when they race through in July.

Tourist moments aside, the rigours of high-altitude training camps cannot be underestimated. While his teammates' racing calendars may limit which riders are available to join Cadel, it is imperative that the riders who do accompany him are able and willing to climb mountain after mountain with him and match the intensity he needs. Santaromita fit the bill—especially as they are both trained by Andrea Morelli and their programs were similar—and he and Cadel did an impressive amount of training leading up to the Dauphiné.

Although other riders were welcome to attend the camps, in 2011 most of Cadel's teammates had other commitments, such as the Giro d'Italia, Tour of California, Tour de Suisse or their respective national road titles a week before the Tour; many were also still in need of rest periods after a busy campaign in the European spring classics. There are benefits in small numbers, though: having a small, focused group at training camps means there's less conflict in training regimes, and more flexibility for travelling and planning.

• • •

A degree of flexibility is needed to fit route reconnaissance in around the training camps and racing schedules. If time permits, most riders like to go and see the important stages, but there is only so much time they can take out of racing and a regular, consistent training routine. And some of the stages are difficult to get to, so the fatigue of travel can outweigh the benefits of a reconnaissance. On other occasions riders find that even if they conduct a careful reconnaissance, the weather and the racing conditions on the day can render it a waste of time. Sometimes the crowds at the Tour are so big they can actually block the wind that otherwise may have had a small effect on the race.

Cadel started the Critérium du Dauphiné fatigued after a big block of training that included a 12-day high-altitude camp, and he was suffering from some allergy problems; but, because it was a race in which he had finished second three times before, he was still regarded as one of the main favourites. He was, however, realistic about his chances when racing on tired 'training legs'—though he hoped his legs would return for the final stage time trial in Grenoble, which would be held on the exact same course as the Tour's final time trial. Does high altitude training work? 'You hope so ... if you have done it right', Cadel told the media:

> [At] altitude you can't train as hard. Your recovery is compromised. Sometimes you take one step back to take two steps forwards. But physiologically, your efficiency improves because of the adaption. That's the whole idea, and you hope it works.

Meanwhile, Briton Bradley Wiggins was in excellent form and primed for an attempt at winning the French race. In 2009 the former track-pursuiter had raised hopes in his home country of a Tour podium finish when he placed fourth, but had disappointed in 2010 when he finished 24th.

Wiggins knew that he had to produce an impressive ride in the race to shore up the faith of his British Sky team in his bid for the 2011 Tour. And Wiggins delivered. He rode superbly, and his team responded accordingly, in a manner that raised expectations in Britain that he was the real deal.

For some Tour contenders, the Dauphiné is a bit of a trial run. A potential hazard for any Tour contender going all-out for a win in a race as prestigious as the Critérium du Dauphiné is that the effort can tap into vital reserves best saved for the Tour, or it could even lead that rider and team to expose too much of their strengths to their rivals.

Cadel races to win, but sometimes, even though it is against the competitive spirit, holding back at certain times is necessary. When a rider is there to win they can—and often have to—push themselves more when they're defending the lead. They dig a bit deeper, and there's a danger in that.

Cadel would no doubt have savoured a victory, but being in the winning frame of mind by the end of the Critérium du Dauphiné is often more important than a victory heading into the Tour. After the results of 2011, coming second—for the fourth time in succession—was fine. He wasn't concerned. Unfortunately for Wiggins, he and Cadel didn't have the opportunity to make a comparison at the end of the Tour.

The Critérium du Dauphiné has long been regarded as a dress-rehearsal for the Tour because it often passes some of the Alpine mountains in the upcoming Tour, but in 2011 the most important stage for Cadel was the Critérium du Dauphiné's 42-kilometre stage 3 time trial in Grenoble. It was a challenging route highlighted with corners, hills and narrow roads, the same as the penultimate 19th stage of the Tour. On the morning of the Critérium du Dauphiné time trial, Cadel and John Lelangue carried out their own reconnaissance of the race route in the car.

The time trial was later won by German Tony Martin (HTC-Highroad), who for several years has been one of the most improved riders against the clock. By the year's end, he was arguably the best in the discipline, having won the same stage in the Tour, Paris–Nice, the Tour de Romandie and the world title in Copenhagen. Cadel, also a strong time-triallist, placed sixth at 1 minute 20 seconds to Martin, and would later place second to him in the Tour on the same course at 7 seconds.

Many believe that in time Martin will become a challenger for the general classification (GC) in the grand tours. In 2011, he was winning time trials and beating Fabian Cancellara, and general classification riders probably used him as a point of reference leading into the Tour—it seemed clear that if you beat him you were probably going to beat all the others. Unlike GC riders, who need to be in top form every day of a race, time-trial specialists can take it a bit easier and recover for one or two days before a time trial.

For Cadel, though Martin may have been a useful barom-eter, more important was the opportunity the Critérium du Dauphiné time trial gave him to race on the same route he would ride in the Tour—to see the course at race speed, on closed roads.

6

THE MAKING OF A TOUR TEAM

One of the biggest challenges Cadel Evans has faced in preparing for and racing the Tour de France has been making sure he has the best team—of riders and staff—to help him win. His late arrival to BMC may have limited the team's ability to tailor a team around him for the 2010 Tour, but by 2011 BMC had been able to make good use of the lessons learned in its first season with Cadel, take note of what he would need, and recruit accordingly.

Most squads that number up to 30 riders usually identify a long-list of about 15 candidates for their nine-man Tour team. The names on this list reflect those riders who are specifically aiming for the Tour, rather than those who will otherwise be needed to focus on another grand tour, such as the Giro d'Italia. Recent years have shown that peaking for the Giro and the Tour de France in one season is too tall an order, but many will race the Tour and Vuelta a España, which is held after the Tour. Most teams don't announce their final Tour line-ups (plus one or two reserves) until after the weekend before the start—and those last slots are determined by results in the various national titles held across Europe, or by the latest medical reports should a selected rider be injured or ill.

As the season progresses, it becomes clearer who from the long-list is best suited to the various roles required in the Tour team. But performances and results give the team selectors—BMC's being John Lelangue and Jim Ochowicz—an idea of the final nine by the end of May.

It helps ease selection dilemmas that some riders who know they are borderline picks will openly declare that they will understand if they miss out on a spot for the betterment of the team. There is nothing worse for a team to have a disgruntled rider carrying resentment for the rest of the year.

A perfect example of this proactive approach is Cadel's Belgian teammate Greg Van Avermaet. He wanted to race the Tour in 2011 but said he would accept any decision and quickly focus on preparing and training for the world road titles at Copenhagen, Denmark, in late September—as well as other later races—should he miss out. It's an excellent mentality to have.

It was evident that Cadel's team was behind him—from the evergreen George Hincapie, who was lured out of Tour retirement after racing for Lance Armstrong in all of his seven Tour wins and in Alberto Contador's second win in 2009—to his domestiques. Hincapie says:

> The way Cadel was riding, I was just really motivated to be as good a helper as possible. I wanted to do altitude before the Tour, which I've never done, and just wanted to do everything possible to be as fit as possible for the team time trial and for the parts where my strengths are, which [is] keeping Cadel at

the front and things like that, which I thought I did a really good job with … and there was hope there that Cadel would win it. We didn't have any assurances, but we thought he was in really good shape. It's better to shoot for the moon rather than sit and wait for second or third.

Cadel has input into team selection, but the final decision is made by Lelangue and Ochowicz. Throughout the process Cadel was kept abreast of how riders developed—for only a handful race with him in every event. Many members of the team he took to the 2011 Tour raced with him only at Tirreno–Adriatico. There is also a core group of riders who are Tour certainties so long as they stay fit.

The hardest selections are the final ones. They're all good riders. They all want to be there. What usually determines the final slots is the course. A team time trial, or a high ratio of flat stages to mountain stages, might warrant selecting good time-triallists or big and strong riders (known as *rouleurs*) who can protect the leader from the myriad conditions that cause so many crashes and dangerous splits in the bunch. If there are more mountain stages, the leader may need more climbers than *rouleurs*.

BMC chose a team for the 2011 Tour that definitely favoured the *rouleurs*, because of the hazards that the race route promised in the first 10 days.

The value to any rider of starting in the Tour de France cannot be underestimated. Besides the opportunity it may present to ride in a Tour-winning team or to help someone win a stage—or do so themselves—starting and finishing a

Tour is a badge of honour for any rider. Some will scrap so hard for that final berth that they know they are digging so deep into their reserves they may have compromised their ability to have any impact in the race.

Team selection can get very delicate. Someone's going to be disappointed, and that's where the mentality of riders like Greg Van Avermaet is refreshing. In the end, the result of the Tour is the best indicator of whether the selectors have made the right decisions.

Some riders sacrifice their own opportunities by prioritising the Tour, such as Italian riders who are required to miss their home tour, the Giro d'Italia, when they are put on the Tour de France long-list. BMC's Ivan Santaromita and Manuel Quinziato were in this position in 2011 when they gave up their participation in the Giro; obviously it would have been very disappointing if they hadn't been selected for the Tour, particularly given the strong emotions that Italian riders have for the Giro. But when you weigh up the publicity a rider gets for winning the Tour with the publicity they get for winning the Giro, there's no comparison.

The actual announcement of Tour teams is a drip-feed. Each team has its own process for unveiling the nine selected riders and the reserves, who don't travel to the Tour-start with the team but remain on call in case of emergency. Emergencies do happen, and reserves are sometimes called upon.

In 2010, Cadel's Silence-Lotto team called up Finnish rider Charlie Wegelius at the last minute when their new recruit, Thomas Dekker, was suspended due to a doping incident that occurred when he was riding with his previous team, Rabobank. But there are other, more bizarre examples of reserves being called to ride in the Tour de France.

In 1988 American Bob Roll crashed into a spectator while warming up for the now defunct 'Preface' (a warm-up event that was not actually part of the Tour) the night before the start. New Zealander Nathan Dahlberg was summoned from his Belgian home in Ghent after having just finished a local 230-kilometre race. He drove overnight to Pornichet in the Côte d'Amour of north-western France and started, after having arrived at 5.30 am.

In 2004 Australian Matt White crashed and broke his collarbone after a warm-up ride before the prologue, when his front wheel got stuck in a gap in a television-cable covering near the start-finish area; Belgian Peter Farazijn, who was not even a reserve but was the rider his team could contact the quickest, got the call while watching a car rally in Flanders, beer in hand.

Fortunately, Cadel's team didn't face such an emergency before the 2011 Tour. On 20 June all nine riders assembled in peak condition at the Passage du Gois in the Vendée to start the 3470-kilometre race. The riders chosen to accompany Cadel in the 2011 Tour were announced on 20 June.

Brent Bookwalter

Turned professional: 2008
Tour starts: 2
Date of birth: 16 February 1984
Country: United States
Height/weight: 180cm/70kg

Bookwalter is from Athens, Georgia, in the US, and has a biology degree. Since turning professional he has earned a reputation as a fast learner, but more importantly he has proven to be a valuable and loyal teammate who is improving with every race. He rode his first grand tour in the 2010 Giro d'Italia, riding for Cadel after taking second place in the prologue. Heading into the 2011 Tour, Cadel rated him highly to the *Sydney Morning Herald* in an appraisal of his team: 'Of the young American guys on our team, he has been the standout for me and probably the one that the other guys should look to follow.'

Bookwalter rides strongly in time trials, especially in the shorter ones like the prologue, and in team time trials. But he proved his value to Cadel in the 2011 Tour by helping whenever needed—whether it was towing after a mechanical problem or assisting when tactics came into play, as they did on the Col d'Izoard when Andy Schleck attacked and Bookwalter came back from the early break to help Cadel for as long as he could. He rode alongside Cadel at the perfect tempo, when others might have let the excitement of such a crucial moment get to them and inadvertently ridden too hard and dropped their leader. Bookwalter stays calm and does his job really well.

Marcus Burghardt

Turned professional: 2005
Tour starts: 4
Date of birth: 30 June 1983
Country: Germany
Height/weight: 189cm/74kg

Nicknamed 'Burgy' by Cadel, Burghardt is extremely strong in a breakaway, sprint, team time trial or chase. He's an extremely versatile rider, but his sheer strength is his greatest asset. As Cadel was reported as saying before the 2011 Tour: 'He is strong ... strong. He's proven that he can go in a breakaway. He can do a bit of a sprint. And he can pull in a team time trial.'

His race record before the 2011 Tour backed Cadel's assessment: he won the sprints classification of the Tour of Belgium, rode strongly for BMC in the Tirreno–Adriatico team time trial, and was ninth overall in the Tour of Qatar. In 2010 he won two stages of the Tour of Switzerland, as well as the points classification. He also won stage 18 of the 2008 Tour, and in 2007 won the Gent–Wevelgem classic.

By the time the 2011 Tour had finished, Burghardt had seemingly ridden more time in the wind than any other rider. He was there for Cadel whenever it mattered, bar his one misfortune in the stage 2 team time trial, when a timing issue in changes at the front saw him uncharacteristically dropped.

Burghardt was initially one of the more reserved riders in the BMC team. But beneath his quiet disposition is a popular person with a dry sense of humour that his teammates—of all nationalities—have come to appreciate.

George Hincapie

Turned professional: 1994
Tour starts: 16
Date of birth: 29 June 1973
Country: United States
Height/weight: 190cm/77kg

Hincapie, from Greenville, South Carolina, has many assets that would be valuable to any team—let alone one that is aiming to win the Tour—but his greatest would have to be his experience and vision of the race. 'George can do everything', Cadel told journalists before the Tour:

> Everybody knows him as a rider and what he can do as a rider.
> His big advantage is his experience, and his eyes. It's like
> having an extra two eyes of my own looking out for potential
> problems as well as the way to the finish. He gets you to
> the finish safely. He is possibly one of the most amazing
> teammates I have ever had at the Tour.

2011 was Hincapie's 16th Tour start—an equal record with Dutchman Joop Zoetemelk. He could easily have called it quits after having ridden for all of American Lance Armstrong's seven Tour wins and one of Spaniard Alberto Contador's two Tour victories. (Contador's third title, in 2010, was stripped after he tested positive for the banned drug clenbuterol.) But Hincapie has been inspired by Cadel's presence on the team, and the admiration is mutual.

Hincapie is reportedly an 'early to bed, early to rise' type of rider, dedicated to his training, and has a reputation for being a consummate professional.

Amaël Moinard

Turned professional: 2005
Tour starts: 4
Date of birth: 2 February 1982
Country: France
Height/weight: 180cm/69kg

Moinard is a strong time-triallist and climber—quite an all-rounder, with a 15th place overall in the 2008 Tour to his name. The rider from Saint-Jeannet wanted to join a foreign team; when he joined BMC for the 2011 season he quickly earned the admiration of his teammates, especially Cadel, by insisting on speaking English. And he came to the team with impressive credentials.

Apart from his 2008 Tour result, he impressed in the 2010 Paris–Nice by winning stage 7 and the climbers category. He also rode to a strong sixth place in stage 16 of the 2009 Tour, and placed third in stage 4 of the 2008 Critérium du Dauphiné. Moinard was selected for the Tour team to be there for Cadel in the middle and higher mountains. As Cadel said of Moinard before the Tour: 'He is the star of our climber group.'

He was one of the best climbers in the BMC Tour team, especially on the stage to Plateau de Beille, where he was the last teammate with Cadel and took him up to where he needed to be for the finish. He rode strongly in the team time trial. And when BMC was having a bad day on the stage to Galibier Serre-Chevalier—a number of teammates told Cadel they were poorly—Moinard was the last and strongest up the valley towards the Galibier. Quiet and unassuming, he is attentive and, more often than not, right there where Cadel needs him to be.

Steve Morabito

Turned professional: 2006
Tour starts: 2
Date of birth: 30 January 1983
Country: Switzerland
Height/weight: 187cm/73kg

Morabito is a rider who had the ability to pursue his own general classification, and has done so in races smaller than the Tour—such as the 2010 Tour of Switzerland, where he was fourth overall. He and Cadel have forged a friendship, and they rode the final Tour training camp together. Morabito does a lot of road-map research to find secret locations where they can be based during their training camps.

Morabito started the Tour with form: he placed ninth in the Tour of California, fifth in the Giro del Trentino, and second in the Swiss national road championships one week before the start. Australians will know Morabito; in the 2010 Herald Sun Tour of Victoria, he won two stages and finished second overall. As Cadel told the media before the 2011 Tour began:

> He was picked for the team time trial, but also for the middle mountains, and if he is on a good day for the higher mountains as well. He is similar to Moinard and also a part of our climber group.

Morabito vindicated his selection for the Tour—he was strong in the team time trial, and rode well for Cadel in the mountains. On the bad day to Galibier Serre-Chevalier, Morabito rode superbly.

Manuel Quinziato

Turned professional: 2002
Tour starts: 6
Date of birth: 30 October 1979
Country: Italy
Height/weight: 185cm/77kg

Nicknamed 'Manolo' or 'Quinzy', Quinziato is a lot like Hincapie as a rider. Not only is he very experienced, but he is a big strapping rider who was a must-have for Cadel on the flat stages. Having Quinziato, who hails from Bolzano, Italy, is another vigilant rider watching out for problems. He has a degree in law and he loves music. His press interviews often lean towards music—sometimes he talks about cycling.

Nearly every race he rides is in aid of his team leader, but he has the ability to race for himself in the spring classics. 'He is really consistent and someone you can rely on', Cadel said before the Tour. Cadel knew Quinziato would be an asset in the team time trial, as he rode in the BMC line-up that took sixth place in the Tirreno–Adriatico team time-trial stage.

Quinziato was ninth in the 2009 Paris–Roubaix and Gent–Wevelgem one-day races that pit riders against the unpredictable dangers of racing on narrow, twisting and cobblestoned roads, not to mention variable weather patterns and sudden wind-shifts that can split a peloton—or send it crashing down—with little or no warning. Quinziato's credentials as a classics rider underly his importance as one of the BMC recruits whose job throughout the 2011 Tour included protecting Cadel through the nervous and crash-riddled first 10 days.

Ivan Santaromita

Turned professional: 2006
Tour starts: 1
Date of birth: 30 April 1984
Country: Italy
Height/weight: 176cm/58kg

Santaromita and Cadel have the same coach in Italian Andrea Morelli. They also spend time together training, at training camps and socially at home. Santaromita is from Clivio, and is the teammate Cadel spends most time with away from racing. His girlfriend is also called Chiara, and as well as socialising regularly in Europe, they holidayed together in Australia in late 2011.

Santaromita is very regimented in his training; he joined BMC from Liquigas for the 2011 season as one of the team's key climbers. His job in the 2011 Tour was to be there for Cadel late in the mountains.

Santaromita is the good-luck charm in the team time trial. Until the 2011 Tour, he had never ridden in a team time trial that placed worse than second. In the 2008 Vuelta a España he was in the winning team time trial, as he was in the 2010 Settimana Coppi e Bartali, in which he came first overall. This is unusual, given his talent in the mountains; Cadel was reported as saying before the 2011 Tour: 'He is our most pure climber and therefore he was the least adapted to the team time trial.'

Santaromita came into the Tour off a seventh place in the Italian road championships the week before. However, he was unable to make the impact he or the team had intended—especially on the stage to Galibier Serre-Chevalier, in which he hit his knee on the stem in a fall and then struggled all day.

Michael Schär

Turned professional: 2006
Tour starts: 1
Date of birth: 29 May 1986
Country: Switzerland
Height/weight: 196cm/75kg

Schär, a.k.a. 'Micki', is a good team time-triallist, and pretty good in the mountains too. He was one of BMC's least experienced riders, but also one of the most physically talented.

He joined the team in 2010 after three years with Astana, where his results were modest—19th in the 2009 Tour of Ireland and a best of fifth in the 2008 Tour de l'Ain. The 2011 season was really Schär's first in the top division. And while Cadel rode with Schär in the Tirreno–Adriatico race, he didn't really get to work with the Swiss closely until the Tour de Romandie and Critérium du Dauphiné. Schär underwent a steep learning curve but was mature enough to handle it, and by the end of the Dauphiné, the Swiss rider had earned his place in the Tour team.

Schär finished the Tour as one of the team's core members. This Cadel predicted by the time the Tour started, telling the *Sydney Morning Herald*: 'He goes well in the second half, which is valuable, but also shows his personal depth. Physically he is very talented ... [he's] between the team [flat specialists] and the climbers.'

Schär's raw strength was evident before he turned professional: he was the 2005 and 2006 Swiss Under-23 time-trial champion. When honed with experience, that strength is likely to pay handsome dividends to him and his team.

• • •

So who was the team behind the team? They may not be the finely tuned, shaven-down and peak-conditioned athletes seen performing herculean tasks on two wheels, but the line-up of staff is absolutely vital to one rider—in this case, Cadel—having the best chance of winning. And for any team, the competition to be picked to work on the Tour is as fierce as it is for a rider. No-one—rider or worker—wants to be at home in July.

For the 2011 Tour, the BMC team had a back-up staff of 18 people, plus team owner Andy Rihs and president Jim Ochowicz, whose roles and impact on Cadel's path towards Tour victory are explained throughout this book.

Cadel has a say in the staff line-up for his races, as do most team leaders of his calibre. And while a number of them, such as sports director John Lelangue, will follow him throughout the racing season, John knows that being invited to be on the Tour team is as important for staff as it is for the riders.

There is a lot at stake for everyone. Staff not only get the honour and pride—and bar-room bragging rights—that come with a team's successes, but also a share of the prize money earned throughout the Tour in various classifications and stages. Cadel's team was a happy band in 2011.

Sports directors

John Lelangue

Lelangue attends almost every race that Cadel competes in—usually following him in the team car—as well as pre-Tour training and reconnaissance camps. Lelangue, a Belgian, comes from a slightly different background than the typical ex-rider-turned-sports-director. He has followed the sport from the age of eight, as his father, Robert Lelangue Sr, was a former cyclist and worked as a sports director for Belgian legend Eddy Merckx. He has a degree in management, was an amateur rider and even worked for Amaury Sports Organisation (which owns the Tour) before pursuing his lifelong dream of working as a sports director.

Fabio Baldato

A former professional rider, Baldato is the team's assistant sports director. Baldato was surprised by Cadel's attention to detail when he first joined but, after seeing the results that trait has generated, he understands the reasons behind it and the pair have developed a strong bond. His knowledge of the Italian races and roads is of particular importance to the team when they are racing there.

Manual therapist and osteopath

David Bombeke

Bombeke, nicknamed 'Da Bomb', is the only staff member that Cadel asked to come with him to BMC. The pair first met at Paris–Nice in 2005 on the Davitamon-Lotto team. They became friends and worked well together. Bombeke went to the training camps with Cadel before the Tour that year and has done every year since. They have experienced highs and lows—from Cadel's yellow-jersey feats to more than enough dream-softening injuries.

A vital member of Cadel's inner sanctum, Bombeke also has his own clinic in Beveren, Belgium. When Cadel is at home in Stabio, Switzerland, he works closely with friend/physiotherapist/osteopath, Italian Luca Ruiz. While Ruiz is not on the BMC team, he is a vital member of Cadel's personal team.

Soigneurs

Freddy Viaene (chief soigneur), Trudi Rebsamen, Jeremiah Ranegar, Chris De Vos

Soigneurs play an important role in any team: massaging riders' tired legs, mixing up to 60 bottles of water and sports energy drinks a day, and being at the start line, the feeding zone and the finish line to attend to anything that needs to be done. The BMC team has mostly American and Belgian soigneurs, because of the team office and warehouse locations.

The friendly, talkative Freddie Viaene has been with Jim Ochowicz since the 1980s and his 7-Eleven team days. He has a lot of experience in his job, including massaging Cadel's legs for the month leading up to him becoming world champion in 2009. He is an affable personality around the BMC team bus, too.

Trudi Rebsamen has also been working with Ochowicz since the earlier 7-Eleven/Motorola team days. She has vast experience and is a hard worker whose motivation is as strong today as it was when she started out as one of the few female soigneuses on the European circuit.

Jeremiah Ranegar mostly works with George Hincapie, as David Bombeke works with Cadel. He is easily noticeable at the Tour though—he is always wearing a ten-gallon hat.

Chris De Vos, known as 'Grande Chris' or 'The Fox' was new to the BMC team, but he was quick to fit in. He is another hard worker, but brings one edge of difference to his profession—he cuts hair and has become the team's unofficial barber.

Mechanics

Ian Sherburne (chief mechanic), Antonio Biron (Cadel's personal mechanic), Nick Vandecauter, Jurgen Landrie, Ronald Ruyman

Most teams have three or four mechanics at the Tour—at BMC the mechanics team is headed by Ian Sherburne, who oversees all the team's equipment, and makes sure that it gets to all the right places on all of the four continents BMC races in. BMC will have about 120 bikes and teams travelling around the world at any time, at races, training camps and at riders' homes.

Nick Vandecauter, Jurgen Landrie and Ronald Ruyman all work together at the various races, transporting, servicing and cleaning bikes. Antonio Biron goes to nearly all of the races Cadel does, and regularly visits him at home to arrange equipment for testing in training. He joined BMC in 2011. Besides getting the job done well, he is calm under pressure.

Medical

Max Testa (chief medical officer), Dario Spinelli (physician)
The team doctors' main job is to keep everyone healthy. In a grand tour, if a rider gets a sore throat or feels ill in the

evening they need to see a doctor immediately, and try and return to full health in the 14 to 16 hours before the next stage. Outside of the races, the doctors also monitor the riders' health and fitness.

Max Testa worked with Jim Ochowicz back in his early days at 7-Eleven and Motorola, before working with Aldo Sassi and Mapei for some years. As well as being a sports doctor, Testa is also a coach. He offers a wealth of knowledge for an athlete—health and fitness being the crucial physical requirements for sport. Dario Spinelli also worked at the Mapei Sports Centre with Sassi. He's calm and professional, making him a neat fit for the team.

Communications

Georges Luechinger (chief communications officer)
Luechinger is from Liechtenstein and is a football commentator back home in between his commitments for BMC. He is one of the people in the team that Cadel spends the most time with. They try to use their time together efficiently to be available to as many requests from the media as time allows.

Luechinger's role has been very helpful for Cadel since he joined the BMC team. Contrary to many people's impressions, Cadel likes to promote cycling and is happy to work with the media world, so long as requests and opportunities are planned and time is allowed for them. Luechinger, who has long worked for BMC owner Andy Rihs, helps Cadel manage this, usually making it a productive process rather than a frustrating and stressful one.

Chef

Peter Cambre

Peter Cambre and Cadel got to know each other while they were both in their previous team, Omega Pharma-Lotto. Before Cambre began working in cycling, he used to cook for touring rock bands, including 'The Boss', Bruce Springsteen. It is not uncommon to have a chef on the team, but for the riders it is certainly a welcome luxury. Not only does it allow them to have the food they like and need, they can be confident it has been properly cleaned and prepared. It also helps avoid the risk of illicit contamination.

Bus driver

Filip Sercu

Every team has one or two bus drivers. Filip Sercu, a Belgian, was behind the wheel of the BMC truck at the Tour. The job requires an upbeat attitude and air of motivation—a very important factor for anyone involved in a successful team. Bus drivers not only play a key role in rider support, they are also involved in team security. The bus is the driver's domain and responsibility. The bus itself is off limits to anyone outside of the team entourage—unless they are invited—but the area outside it, where team staff and officials are working, is constantly the centre of attention at every stage start and finish, and wherever the bus stops on the road.

7

LE GRAND DÉPART

On the weekend before the Tour de France the focus traditionally turns to the national road championships in each of
the European countries. For non-European riders like Cadel
Evans, this is the last weekend of respite and calm after fine-
tuning preparations for the Tour de France in the Alps.

On this weekend in 2011, Cadel was in the mountains after
having spent the previous days training there with his teammate Steve Morabito. When Morabito left on the Thursday
to compete in the Swiss titles, Cadel remained there to train
by himself, with Italian soigneur Stefano Robino alongside
to look after him.

By the time Cadel was back in Stabio, all that remained
for him to do was to stay healthy and rest up for the tough
three weeks that lay ahead. At that point most of the work
was done; riders do get on the bike every day leading up to
the Tour, but it's most important to stay calm and healthy.

Compared to some other years leading into the Tour,
it was much easier for Cadel to relax and look forward to
the start. The allergy problems Cadel had suffered in the
Dauphiné had eased, and the team had been thorough all
year. Everyone had done their job well, and that left Cadel to
focus on pushing the pedals, and ultimately, on the results.

An airline strike caused some stress for many heading to the Tour. The BMC team had planned to fly from Malpensa, but BMC team owner Andy Rihs arranged for a private plane from Lugano. A van was despatched to pick up the suitcases, the team got on the plane and were soon sitting in their *three-star* Campanille—complete with car-wash and tyre centre across the street. It helps to be versatile in the world of professional cycling.

• • •

Speculation mounts as the countdown to a Tour begins, as does the anxiety for some; the region hosting the Grand Départ is invaded from every possible direction by anyone who has anything to do with the Tour. The countdown to the 2011 Tour was no different.

Cadel was not the name on most people's lips as the rider most fancied to win the Tour. Most observers and aficionados looked to Spaniard Alberto Contador, who had won the Giro d'Italia in spectacular fashion three weeks earlier. Contador tested positive for the banned drug clenbuterol on the second rest day of the 2010 Tour de France—which he won—and in February the Spanish cycling federation had decided to clear him. The spotlight was now on Contador after the Union Cycliste Internationale (UCI) and the World Anti-Doping Agency lodged appeals to the Court of Arbitration for Sport (CAS).

The appeal, which threw the validity of his victory into doubt, was deferred twice before the 2011 Tour started on

2 July. But debate raged over whether or not the Spaniard should race the Tour—and his final decision to go ahead and line up for the start was not confirmed until Sunday 12 June, after he took part in the Marcha Alberto Contador community ride in his home town of Pinto, outside Madrid.

Also touted as Tour favourites for the top overall places were the Schleck brothers—Andy and Fränk—from Luxembourg, Briton Bradley Wiggins (Sky), Dutchman Robert Gesink (Rabobank), American Levi Leipheimer (RadioShack), German Andreas Klöden (RadioShack), Kazakhstan's Alexandre Vinokourov (Astana), Italian Ivan Basso (Liquigas), and Belgian Jurgen Van Den Broeck (Omega Pharma-Lotto).

The hype always reaches its peak on the Thursday and Friday before the Saturday start, in which time the 22 teams in the Tour hold their last press conferences. Teams take varying approaches. Some, such as Saxo Bank-SunGard and LeOpard hold them at the main press centre, with every rider on the team attending; others, such as BMC, invite the media to attend a press call at their hotel—or, in the case of BMC in 2011, at another team's hotel. Because of the modest facilities at the Campanille in La Roche-sur-Yon, there was no room to hold a press conference at their hotel, so it was held in a plain and windowless downstairs room at the nearby Mercure hotel, where the Omega Pharma-Lotto team of Philippe Gilbert was staying.

It didn't seem to worry Cadel, who appeared with his experienced teammate George Hincapie, sports director John Lelangue, team president Jim Ochowicz, and the very happy and entertaining owner Andy Rihs. While attended by fewer media representatives than the press conferences of his more fancied rivals, Contador and the Schlecks, it was clear on the eve of his career-defining bid to win the Tour de France that Cadel was in a more relaxed environment than he had been in past years.

One of the notable changes Tour observers now saw in Cadel was his calm demeanour compared to previous years—especially before he joined BMC. It was very much reflective of his sense of wellbeing in the environment BMC had created to help him achieve his best in the biggest race of the year. Spirits were naturally high among the BMC team which, by coincidence, got to celebrate three birthdays in the week before the Tour while they stayed at the Campanille hotel—George Hincapie on 29 June, Marcus Burghardt on 30 June and chief mechanic Ian Sherburne on 3 July. The hotel staff were initially suspicious that they were taking advantage of the hotel's generous cake supply by having a birthday each day, but it really was just chance.

Crucial to Cadel's sense of wellbeing was that the team gave him the time and space he needed every day to be on his own—a change helped by him rooming alone for the duration of the Tour. Ironically, this change was something that came through the misfortune of teammate Ivan Santaromita. Cadel and Santaromita were roommates during the Critérium du Dauphiné, and when Santaromita fell ill he was isolated from Cadel to ensure he did not pass on the sickness. Santaromita gets a lot of visitors, and Cadel found he relished the quiet. Though Cadel is quite introverted, he'd never done a grand tour rooming solo before—but he discovered there were great benefits to rooming on his own.

With Cadel rooming alone on the Tour, the team was able to ensure that he got at least one hour on his own each day without being disturbed. To make sure that privacy was enforced, only three people were allowed access to Cadel's room—the BMC team sports director John Lelangue, Cadel's personal physical therapist and osteopath David Bombeke, and the team's communications director Georges Luechinger.

Luechinger's concern for Cadel's wellbeing is key, because he manages Cadel's appointments outside of racing. Luechinger follows what Cadel is doing throughout the whole day, keeping in mind the value and importance of resting and recovery, so he can ensure Cadel's time is used productively. Teams want to be available to all the media, but during the Tour de France every 30-minute block of rest time is very valuable. A lot of sponsors and media managers forget this when they see the publicity opportunities—and it can be a bit hard on the poor rider who has to get the results the next day.

• • •

It helps Cadel remain calm that he no longer reads too much into what is written and said by observers who are not from within his inner sanctum. Mastering that detachment from what the press and people talk about in general has taken time, and has come with experience.

Becoming a 'subject' of conversation takes a bit of getting used to; athletes can feel they are no longer referred to as human beings, but more as objects that may not have feelings or emotions. Cadel works hard to not let his thoughts be influenced by the chatter around him.

Occasionally it can seem that some teams are racing for the opinions of the media. A surprising number of tactical decisions are determined by this. For riders, of course, media reports can reveal details about the course and about other teams and riders. But it is easy to be misled, and the BMC team always races with the mindset that anything can happen.

Before the 2011 Tour started most attention was on Contador, the Schlecks and on Wiggins—which allowed the BMC team to really focus on what they had to do to be successful. In many ways they were in a perfect situation before the Tour started: they had a lot of media presence, but the focus was elsewhere.

Cadel is always keen to use his time wisely—never more so than during the lead-up to the Tour de France and during the race itself—and is aware of the time-wasting potential of large press conferences. In those where riders are standing up in front of the media, many journalists don't want to ask questions, because all their colleagues and competitors are getting the same answers—and everyone wants a one-on-one. As a key rider goes to walk out of the room, they're often met with tens of requests for a one-on-one, and what started as a 'short' conversation can easily blow out to an entire afternoon. For this reason, BMC prefers to conduct smaller and more intimate audiences with fewer riders and journalists attending.

Cadel is not an actor, and has never been known for playing to the media. He doesn't attempt to project an 'ideal image', but presents himself as he is. This sits well with BMC owner Andy Rihs's desire to present a team that works well and functions well; he's more about doing the real thing rather than trying to create something.

One of the subjects Cadel was asked about most before the 2011 Tour was Contador and his chances of winning: not surprising, considering his status as the defending champion, and that he had arrived at the Tour off the back of a victory in the Giro d'Italia. Cadel told the Italian press that he felt the Spaniard was beatable, unless he was at the level he was in 2009 when he won. This was met with amazement; to some it looked as though Cadel's best days were behind him. But knowing what had gone on behind the scenes, Cadel was rightly sure they weren't.

Cadel and the BMC team were focused on what they had to do, and there was no fuss about it—which suited Cadel perfectly.

Stage 1: Passage du Gois to Mont des Alouettes, 191.5 kilometres

Cadel didn't know the roads of the Vendée very well, but he pencilled in the stage 2 team time trial and the stage 4 finish on the Mûr de Bretagne as his first two hot-spots of the race—although, from experience, he must have suspected that danger lurked around every corner.

It's almost unimaginable that days would pass in the Tour without something happening, and there was a feeling that there would be some sort of upset in those first so-called 'flat' days—a crash, or crosswinds. John Lelangue's direction to the team was to get through the stage without any problems, and without losing any time, and that was the focus of the team. At the moment, George Hincapie, Manuel Quinziato and Marcus Burghardt are amongst the best in the peloton at getting their guy through those flat stages and into position, and Cadel got through without any problems. Teamwork delivered him right to the front and got him to a good position for the finish.

That Cadel did avoid the calamity of two crashes in the last 10 kilometres of the 1st stage and re-join the peloton after suffering a mechanical problem (which required his team-mates to sit up, wait and pace him back before the finale) was amazing. It was even more amazing that he still managed to take second place in a late counter-chase of Gilbert, who won the stage. Cadel finished 3 seconds behind Gilbert but 3 seconds ahead of the rest of the field, led by Thor Hushovd.

'I had a chance to go early, but I thought maybe it was too early knowing there was a bit of wind about and I got a bit closed in', Cadel told journalists outside the BMC team bus.

Cadel was aware of the potential value of his 3-second time gain on his rivals. The sting of the 23-second deficit that stood between him and victory in the 2007 Tour still hurts. He often refers to one of Lance Armstrong's books, *Every Second Counts*—when you lose the Tour by 23 seconds, every second does count.

The crashes that marred stage 1 were a strong reminder of how quickly vital time can be lost. There were spills here and there earlier, but the real drama came after the day's three-man break of Jérémy Roy (FDJ), Lieuwe Westra (Vacansoleil) and Perrig Quemeneur (Europcar) with 20 kilometres to go.

As the pace immediately quickened, the jostling for position heightened, and with huge crowds alongside the narrow road it was clear that danger lurked with every pedal stroke.

Then it struck with 8 kilometres to go: the peloton was split by a huge crash after an Astana rider collided with a spectator. Cadel and his BMC teammates were in the front group of about 50 riders, but most notably absent was Contador, who was suddenly chasing to save his Tour—a chase that was made even harder by another crash that, with 2 kilometres to go, split the front group again, delaying Andy Schleck, Ivan Basso and Levi Leipheimer.

As Contador's chase group closed in on the leaders, it got caught up with the second crash, where riders were still getting back up on their feet and bikes. The bedlam as the two groups converged took the momentum out of Contador's chase, and the two crash-stricken groups finished together at 1 minute 20 seconds.

Later the confusion became mathematical as debate opened about which riders of the two groups should be granted time dispensation under the 3-kilometre rule, which states that a rider who crashes inside that mark be awarded the time of the group he was in when he fell.

This rule was a saviour for Schleck, Basso and Leipheimer, who were given the 6-second deficit they would have achieved had they not been caught in the crash with 2 kilometres to go. But it didn't help Contador. The defending Tour champion's misfortune occurred 6 kilometres earlier, so he was deducted the 1 minute and 20 seconds he finished behind Gilbert. By the end of stage 1 he knew that his back was up against the wall.

All in all, it was a bad day for a lot of people—but not for Cadel, who was protected by his teammates. They continuously rode ahead of him to keep him in the ideal position, or get him into it by pacing him back as they'd had to after an early mechanical problem. Having a team protect its leader in the hurly-burly environment of a speeding peloton that could splinter without warning, with everyone else trying to take advantage of the team's work to get in their slipstream, is not unlike cars trying to follow an emergency vehicle to get through blocked traffic.

Many teams have systems that eventually become instinctual, and as soon as one rider drops off another one drops in; ideally, it's almost clockwork. It's a brilliant thing to watch when everyone on a team is firing, but it changes every day as riders' form varies—in the second week of the Tour, Burghardt was so strong he sat in the wind all day and the other riders sat back and waited in case of trouble.

Inevitably, it gets rough in the peloton and verbal sprays and physical blows are shared. There's quite a bit of pushing and shoving, and of course that leads to disagreements between riders and teams. Most of the good riders know the difference between right and wrong and they don't create problems for anyone, but there are plenty in the group that will take every opportunity to let fly at one of their competitors.

As intense as the first stage was from a survival point of view, from there on, with each day that passed without trouble, the approach that Cadel and the BMC team took was one that they repeated over and over to the finish: they were firing on all pistons.

However, there was no hiding his relief—and that of his team—when the stage was over and he had escaped the carnage. As Cadel told reporters at the finish as he recovered outside his team bus:

> It was so difficult to stay in position around all those roundabouts, you really had to be right in front and that's what we focused on. It was more hectic than normal. Everyone wanted to have a go. Of course, I also want to take my chances as a GC rider for time on my rivals or a stage. Any stage is interesting and an opportunity, so of course … that's how I look at any stage. It's not so easy, and every now and then I go okay in these hard finishes. What better way than try and take any time gaps I might get [from them].

Jim Ochowicz, the BMC team president, credited Cadel's teammates, especially Burghardt, Hincapie and Quinziato:

> The team kept him out of the wind, on the front. Every time you can make a gain is a big deal. These races are won by

seconds sometimes: 5 seconds there, 10 here. A minute today is a lot. That's a lot in this sport.

Cadel certainly agreed on that: 'You are talking to a guy who lost the Tour by 23 seconds.'

Stage 2: Team time trial, Les Essarts–Les Essarts, 23 kilometres

Cadel has suffered time losses in the team time trial all too many times, but in 2011 with BMC, the discipline became one that saw him gain time on his rivals. It was a surprise to many, but BMC always felt that it was feasible that they would come first rather than second. And for once, it was others who paid the price for a poor team time trial—in valuable time and the blow to morale.

GC riders want to make time, not lose it. Losing time in a team time trial after months of hard work preparing to be at the level of the best in the race really does undermine a rider's self-assurance, as Cadel found in 2009. He lost 5 seconds in the opening time trial and then 2 minutes in the team time trial; before the real racing started he was already 2 minutes 40 down, much to the detriment of his confidence.

It was clear to all that Contador was facing such an experience, even though the Saxo Bank-SunGard team was reasonably happy with its eighth in the team time trial, in which they finished 28 seconds behind the victorious Garmin-Cervélo. But though Cadel believed Contador could be beaten, he would not have underestimated the Spaniard's mental toughness in a crisis.

BMC's readiness for the team time trial was galvanised by Cadel's wins in Tirreno–Adriatico and the Tour de Romandie, and by his stage 1 finish behind Gilbert. The Tour team was a group of very good riders who had prepared well and were very motivated. Cadel being there behind Gilbert, the winningest rider in 2011, and being able to jump away from all the other GC riders in the finale, probably helped motivate the team even more.

The importance of the team time trial was obvious and that was certainly a motivating factor for everyone on the team. In cycling it's the ultimate display of teamwork, and is especially important for a team sponsored by a bicycle manufacturer launching a new product—in this case, BMC's new time-trial bike. Ultimately, Andy Rihs wants to see good engineers and designers produce the right equipment and his riders put that equipment into good results, proving the products work. There is no better marketing than a successful professional cycling team putting a new piece of equipment to the best use possible.

Cadel told the media he was as confident as he ever had been that BMC was up to the task:

> I am certainly hoping we will be making time on the contenders … that's the ultimate thing for me and that's what the other guys in the team think too.
>
> In the past we have gone into the team time trial [of the Tour] and said, 'Hope we don't lose too much time …' When you are a general classification rider … for your motivation

it is a real blow. The last time I was in a team time trial I lost 2½ minutes.

Cadel was still wary of the hazards of the team time trial, where the favourites were Sky (led by Bradley Wiggins), HTC-Highroad (Mark Cavendish), Saxo Bank-SunGard (Contador), Liquigas (Ivan Basso), Garmin-Cervélo (Christian Vande Velde, Tyler Farrar) and Astana (Alexandre Vinokourov):

> I certainly hope we make it into the top half [of the field]. That would be a pessimistic expectation but I have high hopes for the team. We go into it pretty well prepared, but most of all the guys are really motivated which is the most important thing. It's a short time trial, so if everyone puts in 100 per cent it makes a huge difference. On paper we have got some really good guys. But a team time trial is funny.
>
> You can have everything well organised, then get there and you have one or two little mistakes, and it can really slow down the whole team.

Cadel had nothing to fear. The team time-trial camp paid dividends. It allowed Cadel's team to improve on their weaknesses at Tirreno–Adriatico, trial the new bikes and develop the most effective order for the riders to ride in. In the team time trial, the team's time is taken on the fifth rider to finish, so it is vital every team tries to keep at least five riders together. In many ways, the team is as strong as its weakest rider, because if the strongest riders race too hard when they take their turn at the front they can force weaker riders to be dropped. Teams strive for the highest speed the largest number of riders can keep up with.

To come second was not the disappointment for Cadel that some may have expected, because it put the team in a perfect position. But the result for BMC—as good as it was—was not problem free. Firstly, the team had to endure the intervention of a Union Cycliste Internationale (UCI) commissaire whose interpretation of the UCI's rules on saddle positioning meant most teams were ordered to make last-minute alterations after their bikes were presented at the mandatory pre-stage controls. BMC, however, was the least hindered of the teams.

Some riders are trying to go for every millimetre and every advantage. Cadel and the BMC team look for every millimetre and every advantage where they can as well— within the regulations. The rules are there to keep the bikes a bit under control; otherwise people turn up with all kinds of bizarre and possibly dangerous positions. BMC riders always try to have a couple of millimetres' leeway to allow for human error, because each race commissaire measures differently. What's being checked at the start line of a time trial is handlebar length and angle, seat angle and setback over the bottom bracket, and the imaginary triangle that links the three points.

The incident was not a big deal for the BMC team, but some teams had to make changes to several bikes in the moments before the start. It can be very off-putting for some riders, particularly given the pedantic, methodical mentality of a true time-triallist.

Making equipment changes in the short time between the warm-up and the start can be very disconcerting for riders, and can even undermine their confidence. Changes to equipment, especially a rider's position, before or during a race can create problems, and using untested equipment introduces a level of uncertainty. Changing an elite rider's position is an unknown in performance terms, but is also a real risk for injuries. Normally, time-triallists have a very methodical mentality, which is well suited to a methodical event, but a methodical mentality is not always an adaptable one.

Cadel would not have been rattled by the sight of team officials and staff relaying bikes to and from the bike control to the team bus where the riders had been warming up. It's their task to get the bikes ready, not his; and he compartmentalises his emotions and stress levels by focusing on his performance once the bike is ready to ride.

The reasoning and need to test bikes is widely understood, but many believe greater consistency is needed if the checks are to achieve their purpose. The idea of the UCI is to keep cycling available to everyone so that it doesn't necessarily follow that the one with the most money can buy the best equipment and have an unfair advantage. But in the search for optimum performance, it is the riders' job to push the limits, not the rules.

When it can be a matter of seconds won and lost in aerodynamic advantage, going to the limit might save a rider X per cent; going over it might save X + Y per cent. So if the authorities don't enforce the rules correctly, riders might even put themselves at a disadvantage by adhering to the rules.

The biggest worry for BMC in stage 2 was that they lost two of their strongest riders soon after the start—Quinziato, who was designated to lead the team from the start, and Burghardt. Cadel wore the green points jersey that day and was surprised by losing Quinziato and Burghardt after 2 kilometres. The loss was a timing issue as the team rounded a corner. In team time-trialling the slightest error in judging the time taken from doing a turn at the front to dropping back and taking position in the slipstream of the team's formation can result in a rider being discarded—especially when entering and exiting corners.

The order in a team time trial is mostly dependent on each rider's size and, to a lesser extent, on their characteristics. One rider may be able to do a particularly good start; another rider may be particularly low, and so able to still receive a draft from a smaller rider … and so on.

The ultimate in team time trial is to have everyone a similar height, similar build, and similar positioning, but the team time trial makes up a tiny part of any team's season—most riders race 15,000 kilometres in a year, and 50 kilometres of it might be team time-trialling. It can be a really important 50 kilometres, though. But the main thing is that the riders in the team know each other exceptionally well: some riders move a bit more, some are very stable, some have more experience on the time-trial bikes and can corner a bit faster, and other ones leave a bit of a gap. Each rider needs to know the way their teammates get in and out of the seat and how they move, because they've got to sit on the wheel.

The most important aspect of a team time trial is keeping a regular speed, which is easy if it is a long and gently winding road, but corners, roundabouts and changes in gradient and wind conditions alter things very quickly. At the Tour, riders are putting everything into their respective turns at the front, so any little mistake—over-braking, acceleration—can put the riders behind them in difficulty. Even a small gap in the line can be impossible to close for a rider already above their limit. And at 60 kilometres per hour, small gaps open very easily.

Riding on the front involves riding for as long possible while maintaining the team's speed, giving teammates as much time 'on the wheel' (drafting) as possible to allow them to recover and be fresher to ride longer and/or faster on the front. In a well-drilled elite team, riding just a few seconds on the front can be the difference between getting back on the wheel at the end of the line, or not. As the lead rider finishes their turn on the front, they swing off, reduce speed and re-join at the end of the line, recovering in the slipstream of the others. The experienced team-triallist will reduce speed after their turn to recover, but only reduce enough to move slowly to the last position, avoiding an unnecessary and very costly acceleration to re-enter the line.

In the end, BMC produced a terrific result to put Cadel in a prime position to take the race lead in the 4th stage with their second place at 4 seconds to the Garmin-Cervélo team, whose Norwegian world champion Thor Hushovd took the yellow jersey from Philippe Gilbert. Cadel was 1 second shy of the race lead. Although, wisely, his BMC team was cautious about talking up his chances of actually winning the Tour on 24 July.

Ochowicz's enthusiasm stalled when he realised he may have been tempting fate while talking about Cadel's strong position—third overall at 1 second. Meanwhile, among the other top contenders, Luxembourg's Andy Schleck (LeOpard) was 10th at 4 seconds, Briton Bradley Wiggins (Sky) 12th at 4 seconds, American Levi Leipheimer (RadioShack) 22nd at 10 seconds, Dutchman Robert Gesink (Rabobank) 25th at 12 seconds, Italian Ivan Basso (Liquigas) 47th at 57 seconds, and Spain's Alberto Contador (Saxo Bank-SunGard) was 75th at a worrying 1 minute 42 seconds.

'We will just do the best every day we can. And in the end, if we have done everything right … and if Cadel can just keep it going every day … I mean … yeah … we've got a good chance to, to, to …', Ochowicz told the *Sydney Morning Herald*, then adding after breaking into a nervous laugh: '… to close this thing out.'

Make no mistake, Ochowicz was readying for his team to stake its claim to the yellow jersey: 'Any time you can get the yellow jersey you want it … We would like to have it some time during the race, but ideally in Paris.'

Cadel understandably wouldn't talk up his chances at the yellow jersey. Asked about his objectives in the flat stage 3 from Olonne-sur-Mer to Redon and stage 4 to Mûr de

Bretagne, he joked: 'I am not going to bother about the sprints against [Hushovd]', before adding more seriously: 'It's early days yet. But it's a good position.' But then, when pressed about the yellow jersey, he politely implored for restraint:

Oh! Easy ... easy! We've had a great start to the Tour. It's a long way to go. Let's keep working at it. The hardest tasks are yet to come. This is merely an introduction.

However, Cadel did realise the opportunity that the Mûr de Bretagne offered, even though he had not ridden it before the Tour began:

I've studied it a bit, but I'll be studying a lot more before we get there, that's for sure. Alberto [Contador] is such a strong all-rounder, if you want to beat him you have to take time on him when you can. For two days it's been successful, but it's early days.

Told that he was due for good luck, Cadel said, 'I'm taking time. I can time trial. I can climb. Sometimes it seems I can handle the classic style of racing'.

Stage 3: Olonne-sur-Mer to Redon, 198 kilometres

The Tour had only just begun; but by the time American Tyler Farrar had given Garmin-Cervélo a cause for back-to-back celebrations by winning stage 3 from Olonne-sur-Mer to Redon, Cadel could not have been better positioned:

third place overall at 1 second to Hushovd. And it clearly didn't worry him that some were still not placing him in serious contention to win the Tour.

The BMC team just stuck to its plan, staying focused, keeping out of trouble. And why not? All indicators were that their plan was working very effectively. Hence, Cadel was reluctant to talk up his yellow jersey prospects, although he understood the importance of positioning, as he told journalists: 'Getting into a good position in the final is always the best way to make time, which is a similar sort of tactic we used on the first stage.'

However, some riders and observers started to change their tune and talk about Cadel's ascendency to favourite after seeing how Cadel's Tour had begun.

There is a certain amount of hype that surrounds most big sporting events, and occasionally the fuss can have an impact on athletes' ability to perform. While it is complimentary to a rider's performance, it takes a certain amount of experience and energy to detach from it.

A Tour contender can expect to be questioned, tested and almost even tormented by the media trying to find a new angle—or, often in cycling, a new scandal—to write about. The best approach is probably the insensitive 'don't care' approach—which is the one Cadel takes—but some athletes are a little more sensitive and concerned, which unfortunately can be a disadvantage in professional sport.

Stage 3 was not short of a heart-warming emotional storyline, though. The win by American Tyler Farrar—his first in a Tour stage—was dedicated to his close friend

Belgian Wouter Weylandt, who had lost his life in a crash in stage 3 of the Giro d'Italia in May.

As Farrar crossed the line, he raised and held his hands in the shape of the letter 'W'. And while it was the image of Farrar that everyone saw crossing the finish line, it was Weylandt everyone was thinking of. Before that finale in a hurly-burly bunch sprint, the image most cycling aficionados had of Farrar crossing the finish line in a grand tour was of him in tears and riding with Weylandt's LeOpard teammates the day after his fatal crash, when a mourning peloton rode as cortege in his honour.

Cadel, who finished on Alberto Contador's wheel in 35th place and at the same time, said he was grateful for having escaped the hazards:

It was a nervous, dangerous stage with a fair bit of wind in the final. It seems they use more and more narrow roads in the Tour. It's great excitement, but puts the risk rating up a bit high. Fortunately, George [Hincapie] and Marcus [Burghardt] kept me in front most of the time.

Hincapie and teammate Manuel Quinziato were caught in a crash inside the final 25 kilometres of the 198-kilometre race. 'But it was nothing bad', BMC team sports director John Lelangue said. '[Amaël Moinard and Ivan] Santaromita did well to bring those guys back so they could protect Cadel in the final.'

The BMC juggernaut, led by a fit and confident Cadel and a committed team, was clearly building by the day.

8

BATTLE ON THE MÛR DE BRETAGNE

The build-up to the 172-kilometre 4th stage, from Lorient in southern Brittany to the top of the Mûr de Bretagne, smacked of the anticipation that comes with a major one-day classic.

While it was early in the Tour, the steep slope to the finish line was expected to see the first flexing of muscle from the overall contenders, and no rider was more primed for the showdown than Cadel Evans. Most eyes, however, were still on Belgian Philippe Gilbert, who was enjoying an incredible season that already included a historic run of wins in the Flèche-Wallonne, Liège–Bastogne–Liège and Amstel Gold Race one-day classics in April.

Cadel had Gilbert pegged as the rider to beat, but it was Cadel himself who ended up being the rider to beat. His stage 4 win in a photo finish over Alberto Contador, who initially thought he had won and raised his arm in victory, was a highlight of the Tour, coming as it did after Cadel had suffered a mechanical problem near the finish.

BMC's plan for the Tour was to avoid problems, but if problems happened, to be ready and overcome them together as a team. As it happened, their performance in stage 4 was one of the best efforts of teamwork ever seen in racing—and the work of his teammates, and the quick-thinking sense of George Hincapie and strongman Marcus Burghardt, were decisive factors in Cadel's eventual success.

The stage was raced in the heavy rain that became characteristic of the 2011 Tour de France. At about 15 kilometres to go, Cadel had to change his bike. Someone had run into his derailleur from behind, and although it was still partly functioning, it was not working quite well enough for the task ahead. George Hincapie, known for his experience and his ability to be calm under pressure, convinced Cadel to stop and change his bike—something Cadel's nerves on the day might have led him to delay.

It is in moments like these that riders see their whole Tour preparation flashing before their eyes. But teammate Marcus Burghardt was determined to lead Cadel back to the group after the bike change. The whole peloton was strung out in front of them—190 of the best bike riders in the world, on a tiny road, all wanting to be at the front for the upcoming section of crosswind. Cadel got behind Burghardt, who expertly parted the peloton and led him right back to the front in a matter of minutes. He went from 196th to 10th in about a kilometre, after all day in the forest trying to hold position. It was an incredible thing to see—Cadel being catapulted down the side of the bunch on Burghardt's wheel—and explains why Burghardt is sometimes called 'Bulldozer'. When they had made it back to the front, they weren't the only ones having a hard time. Despite the difficulties, Cadel was the only leader left with a teammate.

As Hincapie explains, the way BMC team rode then and throughout the rest of that first nervous week—forcing space in the peloton to protect Cadel, even if it meant annoying the sprinters' teams when it came to the fight for stage wins in the bunch sprints—was deliberate:

Every day you had a feeling that you're going to crash. You were scared some days, but more focused on staying in the front, and when the stuff got really hectic … well, we didn't make any friends in the first 10 days. People were pissed at us because we were always together, and we were kind of annoying. We were coming through and we'd stick in the front, next to the team that was pulling—I mean everybody was mad at us.

That's what it takes. I kept telling the guys, 'We're not here to make friends, we're here to keep Cadel in the front. We're going to keep him in position and we're going to keep pissing people off, it's inevitable'. But that's what you've got to do. They swear at the younger guys, but I'm okay. They don't swear at me.

I got hammered when I was young. Some of the guys up there would crush me. They were terrifying. Any little mistake you make, you hear about it for 30 minutes after. It's nice not to have to go through that anymore, but I'm not the type of rider that does that to others. It was a difficult period, but it's part of a learning curve. You need it in the sport to get it right; and to learn how important positioning is and where you are in the peloton. It can make or break careers.

The assertive manner in which BMC rode was clear earlier in the stage; Brent Bookwalter and Amaël Moinard spent a lot of time riding at the front, setting the tempo while the others protected Cadel. Ahead of them then was a breakaway of five riders, who were all eventually caught before the dramatic finale. For BMC the effort in the chase was energy used early but, Bookwalter says, it was a price worth paying:

Each day ... the idea was, 'Cadel, Cadel, Cadel, preserve Cadel ... look for opportunities for Cadel'. We hoped for some luck and were fortunate not to have a lot of unlucky instances, but in some ways you make your luck: staying in the front and out of trouble is not free; it comes at a cost, a pretty heavy cost at times. But we had the team that could cash in on their strengths there.

Amaël and I rode a big chunk in the middle of the race right in front, dropped off and then worked to keep the break in check. We were criticised for that. We didn't have to do that ... but when Cadel came through and won the stage it was energy well spent. It also gave the team confidence, like 'take charge, commit a guy for the chase'—and then we still had guys at the end that could pull them back when Cadel had his mechanical problem.

When Cadel had his mechanical problem, his team came to the fore after he changed bikes to ensure he could still win the stage, and he could forge ahead knowing that his team was still behind him. They showed that in a remarkable display of physicality. Hincapie, the tactical ringmaster on the team, explains how he rallied the troops and they found a pathway through the bunch for Cadel to get back near the leaders:

> You look for the smallest hole and go up it, but it's tricky when you're going with somebody else. You've got to go and lean a little bit so there's more room for the guy behind you to come through. Burgy's really good at that. That day I followed them up, because if you tried to do with it with only two riders it would screw Cadel if he lost one of us. I was behind to keep people from jumping in on him and in case I needed to take over from the person in front of him pulling. I also knew they needed me for the last couple of kilometres to finish off, so I was also conserving a little bit of energy. Burgy, when he did his job, was done.

Hincapie spoke continuously with Cadel through these moments. It was imperative that Cadel understood what his tactics were and that he had full faith in them. But after 18 years in the professional peloton, few would have argued with Hincapie's *mode d'emploi*:

> [The guys] really respect my sense in the peloton. I can feel when people start to get nervous. I tell the guys to get together. They listen. Even John, but he doesn't feel it when it's going on in the peloton, so they rely on my being there. I'm not just a rider. They rely on my race call sometimes. Over the last 15 years, whenever the peloton has shattered

I've pretty much always been there. If it's a crosswind or something—not in the mountains, of course—but where it's sketchy—a small road or something—I'll be there.

With Cadel finally positioned where he needed to be for the final climb to the finish, the responsibility was then on him to repay the team's efforts with a strong result. A flurry of attacks went from the front group, but it was one by Contador in the lead-in to the final kilometre that split it definitively. Norwegian Thor Hushovd was the first to be dropped, but the pace eased slightly after Cadel and several others reeled in Contador, and the Norwegian managed to re-join.

But then Belgian Jurgen Van Den Broeck (Omega Pharma-Lotto) attacked, and soon after Cadel chased down that move he found himself in front as the road flattened; he was racing into an energy-sapping headwind. He had committed his final burst, and had no choice but to push through right to the finish and hope that, somehow, he had enough to cross the line first.

It was an objective that appeared fraught with danger as Contador charged back. They had a throw for the line and it was in the throw that Cadel won it. The victory represented years and years of experience put to good use at the right moment:

It's a big surprise. I still quite can't believe it myself. It was an incredible finale—to beat Contador in a situation like that is very pleasing. With 15 kilometres to go I think someone crashed into my rear derailleur, and I had to change bikes. Marcus Burghardt helped me out … he is my hero today.

The impact of Cadel's win was significant. It was a boost for him and his team. It was a blow to Contador and to other Tour contenders, such as Wiggins and Andy Schleck, on whom Cadel gained 6 seconds and 8 seconds respectively.

It was Cadel's first win on the race since he was handed victory for the 2007 stage 13 time trial after Alexandre Vinokourov was disqualified for doping. Cadel had also become the first Australian to take the red-and-white polka-dot jersey of the King of the Mountains climbers' competition. It was early days yet, but Cadel's feat was a very clear statement of intent.

Back in the BMC team bus, Cadel's teammates were all recounting the drama in which they'd played such a huge role, and celebrating a day that rewarded them with the stage win, his time gain and a continued crash-survival rate of 100 per cent.

BMC sports director John Lelangue, following the stage in the team car, says the win by Cadel, and the way he and the team responded to the mechanical problem so late in the race, was pivotal to how well they rode in the days ahead:

It was important for the confidence of the team. Not only for him. Since they began the Tour they did a really good job, but they did in that day, particularly, because we had to change Cadel's bike with 15 kilometres to go—and we didn't panic. That we still won the stage and Cadel also took some time over the others was a relief ... it proved we were doing a good job and were in good condition.

The finish was so close on the line that there was some initial uncertainty about the result. Journalists ran to Contador because he raised his hand in victory, but Cadel waited for the official results. Amongst the post-race scrum, hearing the official confirmation is almost like winning the sprint a second time.

The post-stage pandemonium went overboard when people started telling Cadel that he had also taken the yellow jersey from Hushovd; but many had underestimated the strength of the Norwegian world champion's magnificent come-from-behind finish on the last climb. Hushovd, known as the 'God of Thunder', is a comparatively large and bulky rider who on his previous teams was a bunch sprinter and a regular contender for the green points-competition jersey, rather than the strong classics-style rider that he was becoming. But it pays to never underestimate anyone in the Tour—or underestimate what can happen in a single day in the race.

After stage 8 of the 2007 Tour de France, Cadel was told that he had taken the yellow jersey, only to discover it would go to the Danish rider Michael Rasmussen. He could not understand how it was possible—he was sure Rasmussen had the jersey for at least 40 seconds. Cadel was taken to a caravan behind the podium, international television and print media were assembled, and then he was told they had made a mistake. A very disappointing one!

Cadel had been beaten by Contador in the 2007 Tour, and beating Contador—and the likes of Gilbert, Vinokourov, Wiggins and brothers Andy and Fränk Schleck—added gloss to the win on the Mûr de Bretagne. But, unlike many, Cadel would not have been surprised by the strong finish by Hushovd, having seen the former sprinter's improvement in climbing at the Critérium du Dauphiné.

As dusk fell over Brittany and Cadel began to absorb his triumph, it was clear that the stage had prompted every contender to test themselves, and that their responses had provided the first real form-guide on which to try and anticipate any upcoming challenges of the 2011 Tour de France. Although, the reactions of Cadel's major rivals differed—whether it was through denial or bluff, or belief that it was still too early in the Tour to say their winning hopes were compromised.

One thing that Contador's aggressive finish indicated was that he was going to fight all the way to defend his title; he'd moved up from 69th to 41st place overall, but was still at 1 minute 42 seconds to Hushovd. In second place overall was Cadel at 1 second, followed by Fränk Schleck at 4 seconds.

Asked about Cadel and the threat he posed at this point in the Tour, Contador said:

It's too early to say if Evans is the strongest rival, because it wasn't that steep of a climb. I'm feeling the Giro in my legs and we'll see if I can get through this first week and then we'll see how things stack up. My other rivals didn't race the Giro, so they perhaps have that advantage on me.

Contador said he was still in a positive state of mind:

It's an important day for my morale and the morale of my team. We started this race with some bad luck and today we took advantage of the opportunity. It's only a few seconds, but any time you can take back is important. It's never easy to take on rivals like Andy [Schleck]. To take 8 seconds on Andy in 1 kilometre is something incredible, something that we didn't manage to do in the team time trial. It was up to me to shake up the race, so that perhaps cost me a little in my chances for the stage victory.

I am a little bit angry to come so close because the team did a great job for me and winning is always something to celebrate.

Schleck played down the impact of having his advantage on Contador cut back to 1 minute 30 seconds:

I prefer a mountain that's longer and harder. I don't have the same punch that some of these guys have on a finish like that. Contador had some bad luck on the first day, it's not a surprise what he did today. He's here to win, but for us, it's been a good start to the Tour.

Contador's aggressive riding did not go unnoticed by others in the peloton, either. 'I was riding at the front to protect Bradley [Wiggins] and Contador clearly showed that he has the legs', said British rider Geraint Thomas (Sky). 'Contador put a lot of guys in the hurt-box.'

One rider that stood out on the stage but didn't rate as a potential Tour winner—just yet—was Van Den Broeck, who made an impressive attack on the finishing climb. It's unclear whether he has it to be a contender for the podium, but he has already once finished fourth (in 2010), and at his age it would be normal to continue improving.

As night fell, Cadel and the team felt relief at having again finished a Tour stage without time losses or injury from crashes. Every second won is a good thing, as is every day that passes without problems, but there was still a long way to go. And Cadel remained typically calm and resolute, not making too much of his gain, telling reporters:

> Our goals are always towards [overall] classification. That will be done in the last 10 days. Anywhere we can get time is always a bonus for the confidence and for the team.

The one difference this time was that Cadel tried to play down the significance of his time gain: 'The time today is just a few seconds. I don't think that these small differences [to Schleck, Wiggins] will mean much when we get to Paris.'

STAGE FRIGHT

Cadel Evans could have been forgiven for wondering if there were any perks for being first across the line in a Tour stage. As the dusk on a wet and grey day began to turn into the blackness of night, he sat in a BMC team car near the finish line at Mûr de Bretagne long after most spectators, the media, and even the race entourage had left.

As the stage winner, he had to undergo a mandatory drug test, which he did without trouble; but so too did teammate George Hincapie, as one of the randomly selected riders chosen on every stage. Trouble was, it was taking Hincapie a lot longer to provide the required urine sample than he planned. The team doctor, Max Testa, was with Hincapie in the drug-testing cabin. The sun was going down, and everyone wanted to leave, but when a rider is dehydrated, there is not much else to do but wait.

Cadel is tested rigorously throughout the season in regular mandatory anti-doping controls and impromptu in- and out-of-competition checks; the first time he was made to produce a urine sample was as a 17-year-old mountain biker, so he has become accustomed to the process.

Riders are required to undergo base urine and blood tests for their biological passports; any variations between the data recorded and previous tests can indicate to the sport's world governing body, the Union Cycliste Internationale (UCI), if a rider should be suspected of illegal activity.

Professional cyclists are possibly tested more often than any other athletes, mostly because of the sport's history. Riders are subject to unannounced testing by the anti-doping authorities in between and during races. And in order for riders to comply with the regulations, they must record their daily location on an official database so the same anti-doping testers know where to find them. Cadel might be tested up to 30 times per season, in and out of competition; the number varies depending on race results and expectations. Every rider has four or five base tests a year—every three months—and Tour contenders receive a particular focus in the lead-up to the Tour.

The procedure can change so as to limit the ability of a rider to cheat the tests—especially when it comes to the actual supply of a urine sample, which testers must watch. Some riders have reportedly tried to drop a substance into their urine as they pass it, to mask illegal drugs.

The procedure is quite strict, as a small problem can end an athlete's career. The rules are constantly changing and in each country the rules are slightly different: wash your hands, don't wash your hands; wash your hands with soap, wash your hands without soap; don't go too fast. It is a way to keep up with and adapt to different methods of cheating. Even a drop of soap in a urine sample can render a sample unusable—a convenient 'out' for a drug cheat.

Other than the time inconvenience, particularly at home if they have a plane to catch or an appointment that cannot be delayed, most riders are happy to do their part for the fight against drugs in sport.

9

UNFORESEEN DANGERS

The next seven stages of the 2011 Tour de France reminded Cadel Evans of the dangers that lurked in almost every pedal stroke—and they ranged from the inevitable early crashes that would end some stars' hopes, to the unexpected dark-horse threat posed by the French rider Thomas Voeckler.

As with most Tours de France, nerves and tension were responsible for a lot of crashes; but in 2011 the crashes continued into the second week. By the time nine stages had passed, 18 riders were out of the race, among them overall contenders such as Bradley Wiggins, Levi Leipheimer, Alexandre Vinokourov and Robert Gesink. There was conjecture as to whether this was any different to most years. It could only have grated on Cadel and his supporters that some were saying the Tour was compromised by crashes having ruled out so many big names: in 2010 he and American Lance Armstrong, then in his second and last Tour since his comeback in January 2009 at the Tour Down Under, had farewelled their Tour-winning hopes because of crashes.

It was also argued that the apparent increase in the number of crashes was more a reflection of the increase in media coverage and its ability to capture more and more of the drama—that is, that there weren't more crashes, just more journalists.

It used to be that one crash was caught by television cameras, when there were nine others that same day. The crashes that weren't captured on film were forgotten, even though many resulted in riders being hospitalised, their Tour hopes gone. Now almost every aspect of the Tour de France is on television, talked about and debated. There are more journalists to interview riders, and more avenues for riders to communicate their views and opinions.

In the last few years, it seems the Tour is choosing smaller roads in the middle stages, even though it is intensifying the helter-skelter nature of flatter stage finishes. Sometimes stages finish out of town on the Route Nationale, apparently to avoid the potentially dangerous congestion of an inner-city or town finish—regardless of the tight roads in villages they race through beforehand.

Many suspect that this is aimed at creating more excitement. Excitement also creates nervous riders, which can result in a dangerous peloton. Nervous riders have more trouble concentrating; as a long-haul truck driver would know, concentration takes energy. When you're riding your bike and you're 5 centimetres behind the wheel in front all day, in a big group, the level of concentration required is very draining—and as you get fatigued your reaction times slow. A week-long stage race is no big deal for a professional cyclist, but when it gets to day 12 or 13, people start to get very tired.

WIGGINS' HOPES CRASH OUT

Cadel was at the front and to the side of the peloton when Wiggins crashed after a touch of wheels in the 218-kilometre stage 7 from Le Mans in the Sarthe to Chateauroux, with about 20 kilometres to go. His first instinct was to check which, if any, of his teammates were involved and if they were okay. Information on who else is involved, and what the consequences are, is relayed by word of mouth among the surviving riders—or via radio from sports directors, such as John Lelangue—as they ride on.

The peloton's pace is determined by who has been involved. When an overall Tour contender falls, the bunch is not going to ride hard if that rider is trying to chase back. Sometimes riders don't realise there's been such a big crash and that there's such a big group behind—they've got good speed and momentum and they keep going, not knowing what has happened.

The day had begun under showery skies and in strong winds. The peloton speed ramped up to 60 kilometres per hour to catch a five-man attack group; Wiggins was placed sixth at 10 seconds to the Norwegian race leader Thor Hushovd (Garmin-Cervélo). He was close to the front when he fell after 182 kilometres, in the middle of the peloton, causing a split that left about 60 riders in front.

All of a sudden many riders near Wiggins were either involved or had to stop after being caught from behind. It wasn't their fault there was a crash in front of them and it made no difference that they weren't in front, because the crash was right near the front. At that point, race etiquette usually demands that those riders who find themselves out front after a crash slow down and let the group come back. It is considered to be fair and sporting to wait, because inevitably, in cycling, the roles will be reversed one day soon enough.

Wiggins' crash highlighted the inherent hazards every rider faces in the Tour. Everyone wants to race safely at the front, but it has such a high energy cost that it is just not possible. And being safely near the front—as Wiggins was—carries no guarantees; crashes happen there, as well. When everyone in front of you goes down, even the most attentive rider will struggle to avoid accidents, no matter how quick their reactions are.

But Wiggins' sports director at Sky, Australian Shane Sutton, said the Briton had to accept his demise after an early season that had looked so promising, and move on:

I said to him, 'C'mon, you live to fight another day' and will try and bring him back even better than he was this year next year, re-establish himself back on the top rung. He has had a great season until now and we were hoping to capitalise on that form in this Tour, but unfortunately it hasn't happened. It is a fact now: he is out of the Tour and it is up to us as a team to stand tall and think of the other eight lads [in the team] and keep their morale high.

That Wiggins was forced to quit the Tour because of his injuries did not please Cadel at all, even though it eliminated a major threat in the overall race. As much as Cadel wanted to win the Tour, he was keen to do so by beating the very best riders. There was also a tactical advantage in having more overall contenders in the peloton—that being, it would help spread the responsibility of controlling the race tempo even further among the teams. Besides which, Cadel knows Wiggins and knew how much effort he'd put into the year—having been through similar misfortune.

•   •   •

As the Tour began its southbound journey through Le Mans and towards Super-Besse Sancy in the Puy de Dôme and then into the Massif Central, Cadel's BMC team was still being scorned as foolish for taking too much control of the race; but this did nothing to dent their resolve. They isolated themselves from the hype as much as possible. They had their plan and knew what they were capable of.

John Lelangue heard the criticisms, but remained mum about his strategy so as to not give it away. He says:

> The strategy was to arrive at the mountains without having lost time. We had a really good team for the flatter roads, a really good team trial and a really good guy to help for the mountains—in that we would come to the foot of the Pyrenees with a 1 minute or 1 minute 30 second advantage. I don't know we why we would've gone on the offensive.

Instead, misfortune prevailed for a number of other top contenders, with Contador crashing several times in the next days; as well as Wiggins, who left the Tour; Leipheimer; and Gesink. On the stage to Super-Besse Sancy there were as many as 10 crashes. Throughout it all Hincapie revelled in the duty of marshalling the BMC riders and advising Cadel on when to reposition himself in the peloton and when he could relax—not that he didn't know how after his six years at Lotto, when he had to pretty much fend for himself in the Tour as the Belgian team focused on helping Robbie McEwen.

The first year Cadel went to the Tour, in 2005, the focus was on Robbie McEwen winning green. Cadel was just getting a start and seeing what he might be capable of in the Tour. He was often on his own, and learned a lot in those years, though he had a very steep learning curve. He learned to stay focused and concentrate and sit on the periphery of the peloton, all of which was now paying dividends.

But riding with Hincapie, who has an excellent feel for it and more experience, is like having a second set of eyes. When something goes wrong, or Cadel has a moment of indecisiveness, Hincapie is the man he trusts. There are times when they don't agree—such as when Thomas Voeckler took the yellow jersey on stage 9—but most of the time they think along similar lines.

•　•　•

Tensions inevitably boil over on the Tour, especially if an incident that risks the wellbeing of a rider occurs after the finish line and is one that should have been avoided. Cadel inadvertently discovered this after stage 7 to Chateauroux, which took out Wiggins and was won by Mark Cavendish in a bunch sprint.

In the mayhem just minutes after the stage, Cadel was barged into by a race official as he was escorting Cavendish to the podium. Cadel had no cause to expect such a collision—after getting safely through the stage, he was still hoping to make it to the team bus safely. He was understandably stunned when the official pushed through to make way for Cavendish and, in a moment of anger, squirted his water bottle in the official's direction. Unfortunately the contents missed and struck Cavendish instead.

The British flyer was, unsurprisingly, taken aback, but Cadel immediately apologised and Cavendish immediately accepted. However, the incident was caught on film and soon found its way onto YouTube. For the most part it was regarded as a light moment, rather than wrongdoing by anyone—barring the official, whose over-zealous antics were noticed by many riders that day.

Asked what happened, Cadel said, 'Got flattened by the cameraman—usual story', and added, 'that's the way the Tour is'.

But Cadel was not the sole near-victim in the finishing area—as if the crash, which saw the withdrawal of Bradley Wiggins with a broken collarbone and time losses by RadioShack teammates Chris Horner and Levi Leipheimer, were not bad enough.

Australian Matt Goss, then with the HTC-Highroad team, almost had his foot run over by an official car in the chaotic finish area—the wheel brushed Goss's foot, much to his shock.

Those incidents were not the first of their kind. In the 2010 Giro d'Italia Australian rider Richie Porte fell over after a stage; he was lying on the road with his bike on top of him, only to be stood on by a cameraman. Cadel yelled at him to move away.

Cadel obviously has a lot of time for Porte, who finished seventh overall in that Giro after wearing the leader's pink jersey for three days, and won the white jersey as best young rider. Throughout the race, in which Cadel placed fifth overall and won the points jersey, he advised Porte, who in 2011 returned to the Italian grand tour to help Alberto Contador win it, and then backed up for his Tour debut—in which he was again selected to help the Spaniard try and win. With Contador a rival for the overall classification, Cadel was understandably unable to be as helpful to Porte in the Tour, but still checked in on his progress.

• • •

In the 2011 Tour Cadel was equipped to handle the media scrutiny when it eventually came his way. The BMC team came under fire for supposedly working too hard too early, especially after the stage 8 finish to Super-Besse Sancy, when Cadel missed out on taking the yellow jersey from Norwegian Thor Hushovd by 1 second.

Cadel was not concerned other teams would expect too much from his team after their committed approach in the stage.

No, not at all. We were there—five in front—which was a really good number. There were still a couple of climbs to go and with wind, downhill, and rain and dry, the risks are amplified. We took things conservatively. If all goes like this day by day, the classification will look after itself. We didn't lose any time to the main contenders. That's what was important this time. We passed through the day without problem.

It wasn't just Cadel's word either. His French teammate Amaël Moinard had no regrets about their heavy workload, telling journalists at the finish:

> Because Cadel is in a good position on general classification, we assumed the work. [The stage] was still complicated— there was rain, small roads and there was still nervousness in the bunch. We have to think of time [up on rivals], about recovery … But it should reassure Cadel too to see his teammates in front. We're 100 per cent behind him, as he is 100 per cent with us.

Many in the media were supposing that Cadel was disappointed he hadn't taken the yellow jersey. But Cadel's reading of the situation was that it was perfect. He had been there before, and he knows what it's like—being older and stubborn sometimes has its advantages.

Cadel knew the stage finish well—he placed third there in 2008 behind two riders who were later to run afoul of anti-doping regulations—the Italian Ricardo Ricco and German Stefan Schumacher. For Cadel the stage was also the next form-guide, and he was ready for an aggressive finale. By this stage the climbs were getting a bit harder. As the race moves into the harder stages, the selection of riders not losing time is reduced, and the list of real contenders gets shorter. It's not as though the Tour is decided there, but it's an indicator of how things may unfold.

The racing conditions were quite dangerous—there was a lot that could go wrong. But in the finish everyone was asking Cadel, 'You're going to take the jersey today?' He was such a favourite to take the yellow jersey from Hushovd that the Norwegian's Garmin-Cervélo team tried to persuade him that his BMC teammates should control the race.

One rider who really impressed in the stage was American Tour rookie Tejay van Garderen of the HTC-Highroad team, who has since joined BMC. Van Garderen attacked on the last climb—the 6 kilometre–long Col de la Croix Saint-Robert—before the ascent to Super-Besse Sancy, to garner King of the Mountains points—and in that he succeeded. A group of 23 riders hit the last climb to Super-Besse Sancy together, but the stage was won by Portugal's Alberto Costa (Movistar), who bolted away as Contador and Sánchez were looking at each other. But in the end, Gilbert jumped to take second place at 12 seconds, while Cadel was third and leading a group of 21 riders at 15 seconds.

Cadel and Hushovd were both summoned to the finish area, even though there was still doubt over who would be awarded the yellow jersey. They were waiting outside in the rain while the officials worked it out. From years gone by, Cadel has learned to be very careful in these moments. It is just too easy to get sick in a race like the Tour. With so much at stake, it can come across as being unsociable, but losing the Tour is not very sociable either.

The wait was not pleasing to Cadel—and neither was the prospect of taking the yellow jersey, because of the demands that defending it through the Massif Central would have on any team. Cadel received a message from his long-time manager Tony Rominger, with whom he rarely talks about racing, saying, 'It's way too hard to control the race in the Massif Central. No-one can control the race, no-one can take the jersey through the Massif Central and win, because it's too hard'.

That Hushovd was still riding so strongly in the climbs surprised those who still regarded him as a sprinter. But others, including Cadel, remembered Hushovd's climbing in the Paris–Nice stage race three years earlier, in 2008, especially on the last climb on the stage to Cannes—the Col du Tanneron—and to Nice the next day—the Col d'Eze. Passing the Tanneron summit, Cadel had been riding for his Silence-Lotto teammate Yaroslav Popovych, who was in contention overall. Cadel was riding tempo over the top and had dropped back when Hushovd came flying by him on the descent. The extent to which his bike flexed around the corners was enough to give pause to even the strongest rider.

Cadel had spoken of Hushovd's climbing ability before the stage. Asked if he felt Hushovd had a chance of holding on to the lead the morning after defending it on the Mûr de Bretagne stage 4 finish, Cadel recalled stage 17 of the 2009 Tour in the Alps from Bourg-Saint-Maurice to le Grand-Bornand when he attacked to earn valuable points in the green jersey competition. Hushovd bolted away from the peloton on the Cormet de Roselend, caught and passed the leading breakaway group on the descent, and continued on by himself to climb and descend the Col des Saisies and Cote d'Araches, picking up 12 points. 'Sometimes he amazes me how he goes up hills', Cadel told the *Sydney Morning Herald*. 'I remember the [Tour] stage we had [in 2009] where we had the uphill start in the third week and Hushovd went in the break … sometimes when he really wants to he can go uphill.' And Hushovd again proved, on the stage finish to Super-Besse in 2011, that he could still ride uphill strongly when he wants to.

• • •

As if Wiggins' exit from the Tour on stage 7 was not a blunt enough reminder, stage 9 from Issoire to Saint-Flour provided another frightening example of how easily things could go wrong.

The 208-kilometre stage was marred by three significant crashes. The first was memorable for the riders involved and for its circumstances, rather than for any sweeping impact on other riders.

After 81 kilometres, as the peloton was exiting the town of Dienne, spectators were stunned to see Contador ricocheting off the broad shoulders of Russian rider Vladimir Karpets (Katusha) and into the barriers on the left of the road, before landing flat on his right hip and knee.

So sudden was Contador's impersonation of a human pinball, many expected Karpets to earn the wrath of the UCI commissaires. His sports director Dmitri Konyshev risked adding fuel to the fire afterwards, saying: 'I don't know what happened … What's sure, if someone bumps into Karpets, it's usually the other one that gets bumped away.' Contador, meanwhile, said the right side of his handlebars hooked onto the rear of Karpets' saddle.

Then came the horrific mass pile-up after 100 kilometres that ended the Tour hopes of major overall contenders: Kazakhstan's Alexandre Vinokourov (Astana) and Belgian Jurgen Van Den Broeck (Omega Pharma-Lotto) were two of seven riders to abandon. The Tour field was cut to 180 riders, though the future of another Tour contender who went down in the crash was cast in doubt. German Andreas Klöden (RadioShack), a two-time Tour runner-up, was taken to hospital after the stage with a back injury.

As shocking and unfortunate as crashes like the one that involved Klöden, Vinokourov and Van den Broeck are, all in the sport accept they are an inherent risk. Not that that diluted the impact when the heaviest price was paid—that being the loss of life that elite cycling suffered in 2011.

In the Giro d'Italia, Belgian Wouter Weylandt (LeOpard) was killed in a crash on stage 3. During the last week of the race, Spaniard Xavier Tondo (Movistar) was killed in a freak accident in a garage before going out for a training ride in preparation for the Tour. And then, in July, one of Australia's emerging stars, Queenslander Carly Hibberd, lost her life when she was struck by a vehicle while training north of Milan.

Cadel was unsettled by what he saw as he sped past the scene of the crash that involved Klöden, Vinokourov and Van Den Broeck, as well as his BMC teammate Brent Bookwalter, who managed to resume racing. Cadel said after the stage:

They were pretty fast down there. I was leaving a few gaps because it was a like a Pyrenean decent. If you let your breaks

A devastated Cadel falls into the arms of Santambrogio in Stage 9 of the 2010 Tour de France. (Graham Watson)

Cadel rides as the defending champion in the 2010 World Titles in Geelong. (Newspix/Michael Klein)

The BMC team after their 2011 Tour de France victory. (Graham Watson)

Cadel celebrates his 2011 Tour de Romandie win. (Graham Watson)

The BMC team rides hard in Stage 2 of the 2011 Tour de France. (Graham Watson)

Cadel and Contador's Stage 4 photo finish; Cadel pulls through with the win. (Graham Watson)

Johnny Hoogerland after being struck by a television car in Stage 9. (Graham Watson)

Cadel commits to a tough uphill chase without support in Stage 18. (Graham Watson)

The BMC team rides to protect Cadel in Stage 9. (Graham Watson)

BMC team president Jim Ochowicz aids Cadel when mechanical problems strike in Stage 19. (AAP/Guillaume Horcajuelo)

go you just went too fast and I spent more time trying to slow down than speed up. I came round a blind corner and they were all lying there. I saw on the road a lot of riders.

Honestly, it really, really, frightened me, after Wouter and everything that happened in the Giro. It really frightened me ...

The third crash happened with 35 kilometres to go, when the driver of a French television car defied the Tour commissaire's order to not pass the five-man break—Voeckler, Juan Antonio Flecha (Sky), Johnny Hoogerland (Vacansoleil), Sammie Sánchez (Euskaltel-Euskadi) and Sandy Casar (Francaise des Jeux)—and swerved into the group to avoid a tree on the left. The car struck Hoogerland, sending him flying into the barbed-wire fence on the right, and Flecha, who hit the deck and almost brought Voeckler down as they touched wheels.

Hoogerland and Flecha being struck by a car, after Dane Nicki Sorensen (Saxo Bank-SunGard) was felled by a photographer's motorbike as it passed the peloton in a crash-filled stage 6, raised serious concerns about rider safety in the Tour.

Cadel heard about the crash with a car via race radio, but it was not until after watching a replay of it in the team bus at the finish that he became aware of how bad it was, and of the potential ramifications. The sight of Hoogerland being catapulted into the barbed wire, leaving him with 33 stitches to his backside, calf muscle and arms, and serious bruising and ligament damage, was horrifying. It was one of those crashes that leave you lost for words, and it had the potential to damage the reputation of the Tour. It can only be hoped that people have learned from that accident.

The sight of Hoogerland, in tears and still shaking as he stood atop the podium to receive the King of the Mountains jersey, showed how shocked he really was. It was ironic that he was being awarded a jersey after an incident that could well have cost him his life. In Holland, meanwhile, Hoogerland became an overnight star, especially in light of the demise of Gesink as the great Dutch hope for overall honours.

The drama only confirmed to Cadel and his BMC team-mates that their race was ideal: they rode safely in the front. They had some close calls, but they were always searching to minimise the chance of accidents. Thanks to the experience of the riders around him, and their belief in their capabilities, they were laying the platform for Cadel's best Tour yet.

What many observers didn't know then was that, in the fall out, Voeckler was to start an eight-day reign in the yellow jersey, courtesy of his second place behind Sánchez in stage 9. When the break escaped after about 42 kilometres on the category-three Côte de Massiac, Cadel was wary of its potential and the danger Voeckler might pose. It sparked the only disagreement he and Hincapie had on tactics—how to respond when the Voeckler group extended its lead to a maximum of 7 minutes 40 seconds on the third of eight climbs for the day, the category-two Col du Perthus.

After watching Voeckler's results in the early season, and seeing him on the finish into Les Gets in the previous month's Dauphiné, Cadel was not going to doubt Voeckler's capabilities. He went to the LeOpard team and said he didn't think Voeckler should be left so far away. They didn't see a problem and weren't going to help, but Cadel was determined not to let Voeckler have 4 or 6 minutes by the end of the stage. In the end, Voeckler did lose time to the GC contenders, but not nearly as much as most people expected.

John Lelangue, following the stage in the BMC team car, sensed that many had underestimated Voeckler's threat:

Cadel knew it was going to be a really hard day, but I think everybody was underestimating Voeckler. Everybody was saying, 'We can let Voeckler have 8 or 9 minutes'. I knew that we couldn't speed up on those little narrow roads near the finish and get in touch with our guys if they needed us—the finale was a little tricky. So I made the call to George to chase. I said, 'Not a moment to waste guys … With 25 kilometres to go, we have to ride. I don't want Voeckler to have such a gap'.

Hincapie's conservatism didn't reflect his belief in Voeckler's chances of winning the Tour, so long as his lead was limited:

I didn't think he had any chance of winning the Tour, but one thing's for sure: had we not ridden that day, he might have won the Tour. Garmin was riding, but then they stopped when they had about 5 minutes lead. Then we started riding and [Frenchman] Jimmy Engoulvent from Saur-Sojasun started riding and we kept it at 5 minutes. But had we not ridden, nobody else was going to ride; everybody was dead tired. They were all like, 'Whatever, let them get 10 minutes, who cares'. But he might have won the Tour there.

Hincapie has no doubt that Voeckler bluffed with claims he was not up to trying to win the Tour:

To go that well he had to have known he was super fit. He wasn't hanging on, he was attacking and going well … the whole team was flying. When there were 30 guys left on the [Col du] Galibier, five were Europcar.

The BMC team was relying on Garmin-Cervélo to ride, but then they stopped, and that put BMC next in line to chase. It's understandable that Garmin did not try to chase the break when it went away so early in the race, on a deceptively steep pitch near the summit. The latter part of the climb was particularly steep and ideal for an attack, and the effort Garmin-Cervélo riders would need to reel it in to control the stage, when Hushovd was inevitably going to lose the yellow jersey, could have cost them vital reserves of strength for later in the Tour.

Cadel had not ridden over the climb in reconnaissance before the Tour, but he had studied the map profiles closely and knew that the start of that climb was really hard. Just how hard it would be for any team to chase Voeckler's group was clear from the speed at which they went on the climb. Clearly, Voeckler was riding very well.

It was wet and the BMC team expected there would be a crosswind, so Cadel came in, moving up to the front on the outside. He heard a big crash behind, and then they started climbing at extreme speed. Cadel saw a split in front. Hincapie had come up, closed the gap and pulled out, and Cadel got onto the back. There were 12 riders on the top after just 40 kilometres—they went for the King of the Mountains points, and Voeckler followed. Cadel warned his team over race radio that this was going to be hard. The break did get away, and Brent Bookwalter later told Cadel, 'Fuck, the next time you say that on the radio … I am going to sit on the side of the road and start gouging my eyes out'. Cadel laughed so hard he nearly fell off his bike.

Brent Bookwalter had learned what Cadel meant when he says 'hard'. After hearing that word from Cadel on the stage to Saint-Flour, as Voeckler extended his lead, Bookwalter braced himself for the pain to come. Later, he looked back on the moment:

I've done a fair number of races with Cadel in the past two years. I remember three instances where he's come up to me early on in a race, looked at me and said, 'Man, today's going to be really hard'. The first time he said it, it was the day he won the Strade Bianche stage in the 2010 Giro d'Italia—he came up after 30 kilometres and said, 'Get ready, this is going to be a slugfest'. I said, 'Every day's like that'. But that race was one of the most horrific events I had ever been in. That kind of scarred me, and whenever he's said that again, I'm like, 'Oh, God'. I pull my hood over my head and say, 'Here we go again, it's one of those'. That is because if Cadel says it's going to be a big day … his perspective is a little different to mine.

When a selection's made in a race like that and goes, it means there are really good-quality bike riders in the breakaway; BMC was in for a really hard day just to stay in contention. Garmin could probably have ridden it back, but they would have risked killing themselves on a really hard stage—and if Hushovd had got dropped on the last or second-last climb, they would have wasted that energy. So they made a call early on.

Contador was further back, and so when Garmin-Cervélo decided not to ride, the responsibility for chasing down the break fell to overall favourites BMC and LeOpard. LeOpard didn't want to ride. So in the end it came down to BMC to chase down the break, which saw them go for a safe margin rather than a secure margin, because they weren't getting help from anyone.

Cadel's concern that Voeckler was a serious threat was based on the Frenchman's improvement in climbing, particularly at the Critérium du Dauphiné shortly before the Tour. Cadel had also not forgotten Voeckler's fighting spirit in 2004, when he wore the yellow jersey for 10 days from stages 5 to 14 and surprised many with how fiercely he defended it, in particular on the finish of stage 13 at Plateau de Beille, where he hung on by a meagre 22 seconds.

Voeckler became the best breakaway rider for 2011; he isn't someone you want to give breaks to, because he can hang on for a long time. Some underestimated him and expected that he'd lose 6 minutes the next day, but Cadel thought differently. Voeckler loves the French crowd, he is a good rider, and it was a good situation for him to aspire to great things. So Cadel decided they'd keep Voeckler's lead within striking distance. BMC rode, but conservatively, aiming to keep it at a distance that was safe for them, but not secure for everybody else.

When Voeckler became the Tour leader, his overall advantage was 1 minute 49 seconds on second-placed Spaniard Luis León Sánchez (Rabobank) and 2 minutes 26 seconds on Cadel. At another 3 seconds and 11 seconds respectively were brothers Fränk and Andy Schleck, while Contador was at another 1 minute 41 seconds to Cadel.

Observers were speculating that Voeckler would keep the yellow jersey for one day, and then that he'd keep it for two. Some thought he'd lose it at Plateau de Beille. Everyone thought he'd lose it by stage 12 at Luz-Ardiden, but Cadel believed Voeckler was going to make it through there—and that if he had a big gap after Plateau de Beille, things could get difficult. It was unlikely that anyone would let him go in a break again. Normally after a rider has made a break like that, the teams with interests for general classification are more cautious, and future breakaway companions pick up on this. It will be interesting to see if Voeckler ever gets in a break like this again.

That Voeckler repeatedly said after another day in the yellow jersey that he didn't think he would last another stage in the lead led some to suspect he was playing down his chances to capitalise on the fact that most people underestimated the threat he posed. It was a ploy Cadel understood, but Voeckler pushed it too far when he suggested that—as BMC was increasingly becoming the favourite for the Tour—the BMC team should assume control of the Tour from Voeckler and his tiring Europcar team.

10

FAST LANE TO THE SLOW LANE

The rest day in any Tour is busier than its name implies. With teams and the Tour entourage stationed in myriad villages throughout the countryside, the region becomes a hive of activity. Press conferences are held at hotels through the host department, or in the main press centre of the official rest-day host, while riders disperse on training rides of various lengths in groups, or even alone.

In the 2011 Tour, the town of Saint-Flour in the Massif Central was the official hub for the first of two rest days—and the rider attracting the most attention was Frenchman Thomas Voeckler, who had taken the yellow jersey the day before. Voeckler, highly sought after by a French media that had been unable to report on a local Tour winner since the legendary Breton Bernard Hinault won his fifth and last crown in 1985, was more than happy to oblige the demand. He spent his time at his team hotel, riding his bike on the rollers in the garden—which made page one of the French sports daily newspaper *L'Equipe*—conducting television, radio and print interviews, and enjoying the company of his wife and daughter.

The Schlecks also held a press conference at their hotel, after their group training ride with their teammates in the morning, as did Contador with his Saxo Bank-SunGard team, and Belgians Philippe Gilbert and Jurgen Van Den Broeck of Omega Pharma-Lotto—all were attended by a large media throng. Cadel Evans, whose team was staying at the Grand Hotel des Sources in Vic-sur-Cere did the same, but received relatively modest media interest. Not that he was concerned. He was satisfied with how the Tour was panning out for him and the BMC team. He was third overall at 2 minutes 26 seconds to Voeckler; Andy Schleck was fifth at 2 minutes 37 seconds, and Contador was 16th at 4 minutes 7 seconds.

The BMC team was happy with its press conference, and was confident that bigger press conferences were to come: the team was in a good position to win the Tour. Cadel was happy with the gap they had on Andy Schleck and on Contador. His main concern had always been Fränk and Andy Schleck racing together in the mountains—that was going to be something difficult to manage—and they had the big mountains still to come.

Cadel was in a buoyant mood as he spoke on the eve of the 158-kilometre 10th stage from Aurillac to Carmaux. However, there was a growing suspicion that the LeOpard team was secretly plotting to launch Fränk Schleck, who was fourth overall at 2 minutes 29 seconds to Voeckler, because they felt he was their best bet to win the Tour—rather than Andy, whose form was still in some doubt.

Cadel had contemplated the prospect. Asked about the chances of Fränk Schleck—the elder of the Schleck brothers—winning the Tour, and how having them in the same team affected the race, he said:

We consider him [Fränk]. In the mountains the Fränk-and-Andy combination—over Alberto [Contador] at his best—is one of the hardest things to come against in the Pyrenees and the Alps, especially if both are in classification.

But Cadel was confident that in climbers Steve Morabito, Ivan Santaromita and Amaël Moinard he had the arsenal of support he needed for the Pyrenean stages, the first being the 12th stage from Cugnaux to Luz-Ardiden. 'We are trying to really save for Luz-Ardiden and onwards', Cadel said. But as confident as Cadel was that they would deliver, he admitted that there were no guarantees:

> I'm confident in that they are going to do their best, but for all of us—me included—until we get to the mountains, you don't really know how you are going. You can think you are going great but get dropped straight away; or you think you are going bad and you make it all the way through [the stage and] into the final group.

Cadel spoke calmly and unhurriedly at his press conference on a myriad issues.

Asked if he feared that he may have peaked too early in the Tour, he said:

> We'll see when we get to the third week. That's when we will know for sure. My coach and I worked very hard for this Tour and we have planned it very carefully, with months and months of work and years and years of experience. I am really

happy with how it is. On paper it doesn't seem to you that you need to be good, but to stay in front you need to be pretty good.

Asked about the Pyrenees and the Alps and how they may affect the race, he said:

All mountains are hard. We looked at a couple of the climbs and there are some really hard days there, but I think the block in the Alps—when you have such a short intense day at Alpe d'Huez—everyone will be pretty tired [by then] … If you are on a bad day, it's going to be horrible, but it's always hard …

Told of the comments that same day in earlier press conferences by Andy Schleck and Contador that he was now rated as the Tour favourite, Cadel said:

It's a good start. So far the team have delivered me to a great position, not just every day but overall to where we are on classification. [Sammie] Sánchez still has time to get into a good position. We just want to continue as we are when we hit the mountains and keep doing this every day.

Pressed on Contador's knee injury from a crash, and suggestions it may not be as severe as reported, but a bluff, Cadel said:

Certainly, if he had a real knee problem it can be bad for him to race [with it]. I had the month of April out [with a knee injury]. I know how it can be. Alberto has been quite unlucky here with bits and pieces and little crashes that sometimes shouldn't have happened. We will see. It might be something. It might be nothing.

Cadel later elaborated on Contador, saying he was:

Close enough to sense what he is going through ... On a personal level I have nothing against him. I admire him as a bike rider. He is a pretty simple guy—we don't talk much because we are quite fierce competitors. I see he had a bit of a limp early in the race which looks like he is struggling. It's hard to read into it. If you hit the ground ... it can really take it out of you.

On the need for luck in the Tour, Cadel said:

You always need luck in these races, especially coming to the Tour. Most of all we have had some luck. I have had plenty of close calls myself. I wasn't too far back from the crash on the descent [on stage 9]. George Hincapie, Micki Schär and Manuel Quinziato have really kept me well positioned—the closer you are to the front the less guys there are to crash in front of you, but sometimes they crash too.

As for why he didn't go for the yellow jersey when it was within 1 second of him, when asked if he was disappointed he didn't get it, Cadel answered: 'No, no. I think we are really well positioned right now ... it [would have been] really hard to control the race. Compliments to Hushovd at Super-Besse ...'

When asked how the BMC team was handling the pressure of the expectations now upon them, Cadel said:

> We worked hard, prepared well, had a plan and stayed with it. We are earning ourselves quite a bit of respect as well. Any expectations, I feel them in a kind of deserving way. I don't feel any pressure, not yet ...

And so Cadel's press conference went on ... calmly, smoothly and without rush. He was clearly at ease with what was to come.

• • •

Cadel was also buoyed by the arrival of his wife, Chiara, and dog, Molly, the day before, in time for the stage finish in Saint-Flour.

Cadel is often not told of Chiara's visits beforehand, but senses them coming 'when her messages stop coming through', which means she is enroute to the race. He was right this time. She had left their home in Stabio at 4 am the day before and drove with Molly to reach Saint-Flour by 1 pm for the stage 9 finish. She saw him at the stage finish, ate dinner with the team, and left late at night; because so many hotels were full, she found a village where she could stay in a convent that had been recommended to her.

Cadel's reunion with Chiara and Molly the day of the Saint-Flour stage finish added some comic relief to a dramatic and tension-filled day marred by the crash of Hoogerland and Flecha, and by Voeckler's yellow jersey feat. The sight of a smiling Cadel greeting Chiara and a barking Molly, who leapt up to Cadel as he rode slowly through the crowd towards his BMC team bus, brought smiles to all those who saw it. Cadel had heard a dog barking as he crossed the finish line and thought it sounded like his. Dogs aren't generally allowed on the finish line, but Chiara somehow found a way. Some people find Cadel's affection for Molly and her attendance at the Tour peculiar, but he has never made any apologies for the fact that she makes him smile.

On a rest day, Cadel and his team generally have a sleep-in and then ride a one-hour loop together at about 10 or 11 am—on this occasion they rode out from Vic-sur-Cere and into the countryside. The purpose of such a ride is as much to escape the hype and busy atmosphere of the team hotel—where mechanics are repairing and cleaning bikes, soigneurs are preparing food, and fans are hanging around in hope of a signature or piece of memorabilia—as it is to keep the system used to riding and prevent lethargy from setting in.

Cadel usually rides a bit longer than most people do, because his body reacts better when he spends slightly longer on the bike. There's always the temptation to ride more, but half an hour less on a bike is half an hour more he can spend sitting on his bed.

A LEADER WHO CARES

Brent Bookwalter got to see the true measure of Cadel Evans in the 2010 Giro d'Italia and Tour de France, when he rode on despite his overall winning hopes being dashed by illness or injury. Bookwalter got to see it again in the 2011 Tour, when Cadel was rewarded for his toughness by becoming the first Australian to win the world's biggest and most prestigious bike race.

However, it was on the first of the 2011 Tour's two rest days that Bookwalter experienced first-hand Cadel's compassion as a leader, and his ability to lift a teammate from the brink of despair in the aftermath of a crash the day before.

The crash he is talking about, on the 9th stage to Saint-Flour, was not the one in which Johnny Hoogerland and Juan Antonio Flecha were struck by a French television car as it passed them and the others in a five-man breakaway. It was a crash earlier in the day, on the descent of the Puy Mary, that left Kazakhstan's Alexandre Vinokourov (Astana), Belgian Jurgen Van Den Broeck (Omega Pharma-Lotto) and American David Zabriskie (Garmin-Cervélo) among those who were forced to abandon the Tour because of injury.

Bookwalter was one of the victims, and while he needed a new bike—the impact broke his forks—he was thankful that he was still able to continue. But his condition and the scene at the crash site cast a pall over any joy he may have felt. Bookwalter, who was eighth wheel at the time, had Cadel riding behind him and came a cropper when he ran into a Belgian rider who had already fallen. How Cadel missed the tangled mess of body and bike is anyone's guess—but he did. Bookwalter recalls the incident vividly:

I was really shaken up mentally and emotionally. Cadel said he was shaken up. It was like we'd come through a war zone—guys were screaming in the woods, limping back, falling over ... and I had this moment of 'What are we doing?' I was having a really good day up to that point, working well for the team and Cadel. After I crashed, it became a matter of almost not even making it through the stage. I was just having to survive and I was feeling helpless and down ... I had split my head and my back and my hips were really sore. Everything was twisted and pulled and I had a gash on my neck and road rash.

Bookwalter managed to finish, buoyed by the fact that the next day was a rest day and that he might be able to recover. He soon found that was going to be harder than he expected. When he woke up, he was so sore and stiff that he had difficulty getting out of bed. Then, when the team went out for a light training ride, he was dropped. The moment was a blow he didn't need near the mid-point of the Tour—although the potential despair was averted when Cadel, noticing he was struggling, dropped back to ride with him. Bookwalter recalls:

We were on small, bumpy roads ... steep, up and down, and everyone's riding easy. But I'm getting dropped on the rest day. I can't even keep up with the guys on the rest-day ride. Then Cadel drops back and says, 'Great job in the first week. We're right where we want to be. You guys are doing awesome. Just let yourself rebound from the crash, and then we'll get into the mountains and we'll be totally fine'.

Bookwalter realised then that a large part of his despair was a sense that he had let Cadel down because of his injuries, or would do so in the days to come, when he would be needed the most. But Cadel's reassurance and request that he back off and focus on recovering first—that is, focus on himself—for a few days before the Alps alleviated his worry:

I was even better than I thought I would be over the next two days. It was as if the guy who is leading the team—the guy that you're there for—understands you. He knows you're working in less than prime conditions.

He's been in that situation before and ... that's what he's all about, what the sport's about, and the Tour—learning to adapt and endure and come through frustrating situations.

Once Cadel had finished his ride, he spent most of the remainder of the rest day sleeping in his room with Chiara and Molly, who were just as exhausted as he was from their long overnight trip from Stabio to Saint-Flour. In the late afternoon he awoke for a massage and body overhaul from his personal osteopath David Bombeke and, after an aperitivo and dinner, he went to bed early to recover and get ready for the next day. But the team management and staff were feeling quite confident and happy, and had a small party. They weren't quite as bright and sparkly as they could've been the next morning, but they were enjoying themselves and everyone was doing their job. It was also a nice little subconscious pat on the back for everyone on the team.

Winning the Tour is a slow process emotionally. A team might know they're in a good position as the first day passes and then the second day and the third day—but there are still 18 days to go. Even when the team reached the second rest day in good standing, they knew they still had big mountains and a big time trial ahead of them.

Cadel did not go to the party because, apart from needing the rest, he was understandably—and wisely—reluctant to get ahead of himself. He did, however, share the optimism of the BMC team staff, despite the Tour having only just begun and the Pyrenees approaching. Stages 10 and 11 after the rest day were tailored to the sprinters—and then there were the Alps near the end of the third week.

But extra sleep was more valuable for Cadel than a drink. If riders can sneak an extra hour of sleep per day—or at least some time lying on their bed—it makes for almost a full extra day of rest in a 23-day Tour. But that is a lot easier said than done, because of the length of the stages—which have shortened in recent years under the tenure of Christian Prudhomme as Tour race director—and because of post-race transfers and other logistical hindrances, such as congestion on the roads on mountain tops and traffic jams on small country roads in the valleys.

Riders actually get to sleep in quite a lot on the Tour, but the problem is getting to bed early enough. Everyone in the race wants less travel and more rest. If everyone gets more rest and has less stress outside of the race, they can race better each day, which makes the race more interesting and better for everyone.

• • •

Cadel is not a sprinter. Suggest that he is, and he would laugh. But it was not uncommon during the 2011 Tour de France to see him tucked behind a line of BMC teammates

racing elbow to elbow alongside the big trains of the sprinters' teams in the last 10 kilometres of the flatter stages. Not
that Cadel was driven by any false pretence of getting the
better of the likes of speedsters such as Mark Cavendish,
André Greipel or Alessandro Petacchi. It was all a part of the
strategy to keep him out of trouble and in a clearer pathway
during the helter-skelter and frighteningly dangerous finale
to a stage, when it is best to have more riders behind than
in front.

BMC's plan was to keep Cadel as close as possible to the
front of the peloton for as long as possible, but without inter-
fering in the battle between the sprinters' teams. It was not
always easy. Cadel was to be provided with his own train up
until the last 3 kilometres, the mark at which any rider who
finishes behind because they are in a crash—or caught up
by one—are given the same time as the peloton.

The plan worked in stage 3 from Olonne-sur-Mer to
Redon, which was won by American Tyler Farrar (Garmin-
Cervélo). It was just as effective in bunch-sprint finishes on
stage 7 from Le Mans to Chateauroux—where Cavendish
(HTC-Highroad) claimed the first of five wins; on stage
10 from Aurillac to Carmaux—where Greipel (Omega
Pharma-Lotto) won over Cavendish; and on stage 11 from
Blaye-les-Mines to Lavaur—where Cavendish again beat
Greipel. Cadel's placings for those respective stages, thanks
to his vigilant positioning, were 35th, 22nd, 24th and 50th.

There is something of an anomaly in a general classification rider like Cadel entering the fray with sprinters—and
vice versa, when the sprinters sometimes position themselves

near the front of the pack when the first mountain passes under their wheels.

Sprinters have a job to do, and if general classification riders can help them by staying out of their way, or by closing the gap to a breakaway in the final, they generally want to. It's better to have friends than enemies in the peloton.

Sometimes general classification riders get in sprinters' way by accident, and sometimes the sprinters want to start a climb in front before they get dropped. That is when arguments start and things can get messy. In the 2011 Tour, Cadel and the BMC team received some abuse from the sprinters' teams for riding beside them—as if riding for yellow is the sideshow of the Tour. It is not something that riders can afford to be concerned about; everyone at the Tour is under a lot of pressure—very stressed and very, very tired.

Road sprinters take enormous risks, on roads they have never ridden on, with little protection, surrounded by other riders. Many sprint finishes are at the end of twisting and narrow run-ups littered with roundabouts, and can be particularly intimidating. Straight roads into headwinds, faster downhill finals, and sharp corners in the last few kilometres allow some of the 'kamikaze' sprinters to get past the experienced riders, and it often ends up in disaster. And if a crash happens at the front of the group at that speed, it really is bad for everyone.

The 3-kilometre rule is a good one, as it allows the general classification riders to position well and then get out of the sprinters teams' way so they can go about their job. George Hincapie is a specialist at getting his leader through a final safely, but he and Cadel do have different measures of risk. Hincapie will sometimes yell, 'Get back here—it's too dangerous'; Cadel prefers the other riders in the team to stay behind him and save their energy for another day.

Because of this 'unorthodox' approach to bunch sprints, Cadel found himself in the box seat to observe the sprinters at their ferocious best—as did their teams as they formed trains and fought tooth-and-nail for the very best position before catapulting their man in his sprint for the line.

The peloton may be racing at speeds of up to 65 kilometres per hour, and riders may be a touch of the wheel away from crashing; but in all the craziness it's still easy to absorb the brilliance displayed by the world's top sprinters. Cadel makes no secret of his admiration for Cavendish, the Manx Missile whose five stage wins in 2011 took his tally of Tour stage wins to 20. Cavendish's win in the final stage of the 2010 Tour was awe inspiring, as was the teamwork behind it—especially the astonishing final lead-out by Australian Mark Renshaw, who has since left Cavendish's side to be lead sprinter in the Dutch Rabobank team. The finish was so good that it left them placed first and second, with their arms aloft in a victory salute.

Cavendish is remarkable in his ability to withstand pain. When he sees a chance to get to the finish line, he'll be there and he'll hurt himself inside out. He has the speed. HTC-Highroad had the best lead-out in the world; when you have the best sprinter in the world, you have to have a strong team to control the race, right from the start to the finish.

Meanwhile, Cadel also used stage 11 to see how Contador was faring with his knee injury on the eve of the Pyrenees: 'Alberto looks like he is riding well … We will find out tomorrow [on stage 12]. For sure we will find out the truth there', Cadel said, referring to the 211-kilometre 12th stage from Cugnaux near Toulouse to the 13.3-kilometre ascent up Luz-Ardiden. Despite the wind and rain that day, Cadel was calm and assured about the first mountain stage the next morning:

I'll just make my own race, see how the others go and hopefully be competitive or better. I'm all right. I am just trying to stay dry and healthy and out of trouble like we always do. It's a bit of an unusual Tour this year, but now the real Tour starts in the mountains.

11

THE PYRENEES

The Pyrenees failed to deliver when it came to the expected array of absorbing attacks in the 2011 Tour de France.

However, for Cadel Evans, the way the three days in the mountain range bordering France and Spain unravelled was perfect in setting him up for the crucial third and last week. Cadel was correct to be wary about the Pyrenees, though. The steep, twisting, bumpy roads that characterise the ascents used to suit him better than the Alps, but he had also been on the receiving end of misfortune there: in 2007, Alberto Contador won his first stage on the 15.8-kilometre climb to Plateau de Beille before racing off to win his first Tour by 23 seconds.

Since then, Cadel has been careful never to underestimate the impact the Pyrenees can have on the race—especially when it came to the finish of stage 14 in 2011 to Plateau de Beille.

It was the first real mountain stage of the 2011 Tour. Only 168 kilometres, the stage was up and down all day and finished on a 15.8-kilometre climb that is exposed to the wind. Anyone who could make a difference there would make a difference. And of course no-one wanted to lose any time. Everyone is intrigued by l'Alpe d'Huez in the Alps, but it's possible to make just as big a time difference on Plateau de Beille.

Nevertheless, with the way the overall classification was placed as the 2011 Tour arrived at the foot of the Pyrenees for stage 12—210 kilometres from Cugnaux to Luz-Ardiden—there was every incentive for the key contenders to make the best of any opportunity to attack that the mountains offered—though Cadel had no cause to attack, his strong position just requiring that he follow any moves.

At the stage start Cadel was best placed among the favourites—third overall at 2 minutes 26 seconds to the French race leader Thomas Voeckler.

Cadel also led 'Le Tour Virtual'—an unofficial overall classification that ranks the top overall contenders, compiled by Tour observers, eliminating those riders who are placed highly at any given point in time but that they do not regard as serious overall contenders. It is a very subjective classification, but it provides an interesting perspective.

Because Cadel was placed so well on entering the Pyrenees, it wasn't up to him to ignite the race and attack. It was really the responsibility of the Schleck brothers or Contador to do so—if not on the 12th stage from Cugnaux to the summit at Luz-Ardiden, or on the 13th stage from Pau to Lourdes, then at least on stage 14 from Saint-Gaudens to Plateau de Beille. Alas, they didn't!

The three days did not pass without drama, however; on the contrary, the outcome raised doubts about the ability of Schleck or Contador to take on Cadel. And Cadel, in turn, appeared to gain strength with each day—even if the last-kilometre attack on stage 12 by Fränk Schleck, who placed third at 10 seconds to stage winner Sammie Sánchez

(Euskaltel-Euskadi), raised suspicions that LeOpard might secretly count him as their best chance to win the Tour rather than Andy, who finished at 30 seconds with Cadel by his side. The stage was also significant for Contador, finishing another 13 seconds back, in eighth place at 43 seconds to Sánchez.

The first mountain stage is an excellent indicator of, because until then no rider really knows how good they are on a major climb. In 2011 it was the first real sign that Contador was not at the level he usually would be for the Tour. BMC sports director John Lelangue reported Contador's demise to Cadel through the race radio, urging him to put some pressure on—but it was still too early. Then one of the Schlecks went away, which is what the BMC team was waiting for. Amaël Moinard took Cadel to position at the bottom of the climb, and it was one-on-one from there onwards. All of the general classification riders raced a bit defensively that day—because of the wind, the hard day, or maybe because they did not want to show their cards just yet.

While there was talk of Fränk Schleck being a dark horse for team LeOpard, his attack near the finish was not a major concern. BMC was more concerned about Andy Schleck. And if anything, Fränk's attack was helpful—any attack while Contador was dropped put Contador in more difficulty and increased the gap. Observers expected that more might have happened on that stage, but Cadel and his team were just happy to be through it without losing time to Andy, who was their main focus at that point. All in all, it was a good day for BMC.

AT THE FOOT OF THE PYRENEES

Official overall standings (after 11 stages; 1916 kilometres)

1. Thomas Voeckler (Europcar) in 45 hours 57 minutes 31 seconds

2. Luis León Sánchez (Rabobank) — 1 minute 49 seconds

3. Cadel Evans (BMC) — 2 minutes 26 seconds

4. Fränk Schleck (LeOpard) — 2 minutes 29 seconds

5. Andy Schleck (LeOpard) — 2 minutes 37 seconds

6. Tony Martin (HTC-Highroad) — 2 minutes 38 seconds

7. Peter Velits (HTC-Highroad) — 2 minutes 38 seconds

8. Andreas Klöden (RadioShack) — 2 minutes 43 seconds

9. Philippe Gilbert (Omega Pharma-Lotto) — 2 minutes 55 seconds

10. Jakob Fuglsang (Saxo Bank-SunGard) — 3 minutes 8 seconds

16. Alberto Contador (Saxo Bank-SunGard) — 4 minutes 7 seconds

Le Tour Virtual (after 11 stages; 1916 kilometres)

1. Cadel Evans (BMC) in 45 hours 55 minutes 5 seconds

2. Fränk Schleck (LeOpard) — 3 seconds

3. Andy Schleck (LeOpard) — 11 seconds

4. Tony Martin (HTC-Highroad) — 12 seconds

5. Peter Velits (HTC-Highroad) — 12 seconds

6. Andreas Klöden (RadioShack) — 17 seconds

7. Ivan Basso (Liquigas) — 1 minute 10 seconds

8. Damiano Cunego (Lampre-ISD) — 1 minute 11 seconds

9. Nicolas Roche (Ag2r-La Mondiale) — 1 minute 19 seconds

10. Robert Gesink (Rabobank) — 1 minute 35 seconds

11. Alberto Contador (Saxo Bank-SunGard) — 1 minute 41 seconds

The overall classification after stage 12 added weight to Cadel's positive summation of the day: he was now third overall at 2 minutes 6 seconds to Voeckler, whose margin on second-placed Fränk Schleck was 1 minute 56 seconds. Cadel, meanwhile, was still 11 seconds ahead of fourth-placed Andy Schleck and, significantly, now 1 minute 54 seconds ahead of Contador, who was in seventh position overall.

Some observers made much of Cadel's 20-second loss to Fränk Schleck, but not Cadel, who called for calm at the finish. He was still exhausted, as was everyone in the peloton—from the victorious Sánchez to the yellow-jerseyed Voeckler and, especially, the last-placed rider of the day, Russian Denis Galimzyanov (Katusha), who was eliminated from the Tour after finishing alone at 59 minutes 13 seconds and outside the time limit.

'Can I have another hat?' Cadel asked a team aide, between gasps. As a thick fog began to cover Luz-Ardiden he was trying to put on a dry vest, and he wanted to keep his sweat-matted head dry and warm on the 13.5-kilometre ride back down the mountain to where the team bus waited in the valley. But when asked how he felt, Cadel told reporters:

You are never particularly comfortable in the Tour ... right now included. It's still early in the mountains, still a long way to Paris. If the team keeps going every day as it's done thus far—we've really put ourselves in a great position—we [can] get in a great position in Paris. We need to stay calm and see what happens in the coming days. The first mountain-top finish in the Tour, there's always some[thing] that you do expect, some[thing] that you don't ... More or less, I have to see the results sheet.

• • •

Stage 13 from Pau to Lourdes also ventured into the Pyrenees, but the chances of it affecting the overall classification were minimal, especially with the excitement building for the next day's finish up to Plateau de Beille. The stage resulted in a breakaway escaping and Norwegian world champion Thor Hushovd adding a brilliant stage win to his reign in the yellow jersey.

The stage offered a relative respite, as it meant the bunch of favourites could race cautiously on the narrow, twisting roads into Lourdes—they finished 7 minutes 37 seconds behind Hushovd—and minimise the risk of crashing. It was a relief to have an uneventful day.

Learning that Hushovd had won the stage was a victory of sorts for Cadel. By then, the vibe was strong that Hushovd might be joining BMC for 2012. After showing his strength in the team time trial, then in the climbs while defending his yellow jersey, his versatility as a rider who could win with attacks rather than in bunch sprints confirmed that BMC was to welcome a special rider.

While the finish at Plateau de Beille on stage 14 disappointed for its lack of explosiveness, one surprise was that Voeckler managed again to defend the yellow jersey, almost ensuring he would wear it into the Alps. His having defended it in stages 12 and 13 was not so much of an eye-opener; but that he still had it after stage 14 to Plateau de Beille turned heads. Not that anyone expected he would surrender it easily, in light of his stoic defence of the yellow jersey in 2004, when Lance Armstrong went on to win a sixth Tour and Voeckler hung on to it by 22 seconds. But his defence this time was more impressive, considering he'd remained with the leaders up Plateau de Beille—unlike in 2004—and answered every attack.

Such feats are not unknown. Many have ridden above themselves to defend the yellow jersey when they would otherwise have lost minutes. This time, Voeckler knew what that sensation was like, and knew he could race to his limit on the same mountain finish. Cadel had suspected Voeckler's potential since he took the Tour lead on stage 9 to Saint-Flour.

Cadel was not that surprised by the defensive racing up Plateau de Beille, where Belgian Jelle Vanendert (Omega Pharma-Lotto) won by 21 seconds from Sánchez; 46 seconds from Andy Schleck, who bolted away with 500 metres to go; and 48 seconds from Cadel, who led a group of eight riders that included Fränk Schleck, Alberto Contador, Ivan Basso and Voeckler.

In 2007, his last ascent up Plateau de Beille in Tour race conditions, Cadel was worked over by Contador and the Danish rider Michael Rasmussen, who later became embroiled in a doping controversy and left the Tour when in the yellow jersey. Contador had seen that Cadel was reaching his limit, and his accelerations pushed him over it.

Cadel warms up for the Stage 20 time trial in Grenoble as the crowd looks on. (Citizenside/Tim Miller)

Cadel readies himself at the Stage 20 starting line. (AAP/Guillaume Horcajuelo)

Cadel's ride in the Stage 20 time trial brought him Tour victory. (Graham Watson)

Cadel and BMC sports director John Lelangue celebrate the win at the beginning of Stage 21. (AAP/Lionel Bonaventure)

Cadel and his team mates celebrate a hard-earned victory. (Graham Watson)

Cadel and his fellow jersey winners raise their trophies. (Graham Watson)

Cadel and the Schleck brothers — and a fan — on the podium. (Graham Watson)

Melbourne welcomes home a victorious Cadel. (AAP/David Crosling)

Cadel, Chiara and their son, Robel. (Tertius Picard/*New Idea*)

In 2011 there was a bit of wind and the riders were racing a bit negatively. It was a long climb, but never really steep. Voeckler was always there, defending yellow. Other than for the stage result, the lesser gradient and stronger wind made sitting in the small group defending a much safer option. At that point in the race, most of the overall contenders were relatively evenly matched, all contributing to a 'less exciting' race, as some members of the press would put it.

Cadel had anticipated that Sánchez would try and help Contador in the Pyrenees. The pressure was off Sánchez after he had won a stage—his primary objective—but, while not fancied to win the Tour overall, he was a serious protagonist in the race for the overall podium. And once Contador had lost time, any aggression that Sánchez could throw up to press the Schleck brothers, and now Voeckler, would help Contador.

By pressuring the main contenders, putting them in stressful situations with attacks that need chasing, there is always the chance that they might go beyond their limits and blow up. This would prove opportune for Sánchez, as it might for Contador should he be in good form on the day. This scenario suited Cadel, too, for all he had to do—assuming he remained healthy and in good condition—was to follow all the moves.

The demise of those riders behind him, such as the Schlecks—and even Voeckler—would be of no concern to Cadel, so long as he remained ahead of the rest to Paris. Although, as became evident, Contador was unable to produce the form to reap the benefits that such a union would have offered them both, and so the dangerous alliance did not eventuate.

Communications manager Georges Luechinger guided Cadel through a throng of media; as Cadel soft-pedalled to a nearby railing at the mountain-top finish, he told reporters that everything was under control. Many people had lamented the lack of attacks by the big favourites—apart from Andy Schleck—but the stage was harder for Cadel and his rivals than those people realised. The look of distress on Cadel's sweaty brow as he stopped and continued to suck oxygen into his big lungs said as much. 'Under control ...', Cadel began to explain, before adding, 'my foot has got a cramp ... aie, aie, aie ... ow, ow, ow' while looking down at his right foot, which was still locked in the pedal. Luechinger furiously undid the strap to loosen the foot, and advised him to stretch out his leg. The tip worked. Relief swept across Cadel's face. He smiled and resumed to say of the stage:

Things are under control. Everyone says no-one attacked and so on, but you have to consider the wind and the closeness of the racing.

The Schleck brothers are there. They ride all day, they have the yellow jersey to gain and then they look at me to pull for them. Hang on a second, 'I am not here to tow you to Paris'. So many cycling experts said we wasted a lot of energy as a team to put ourselves into a good position coming into the mountains ... and then to see a little bit of conservative racing ... But these stages are hard and you have to conserve your efforts carefully.

Asked what would make the difference between winning and losing the Tour, with 2 minutes 11 seconds separating the top contenders, Cadel joked about the Tour myth that says the rider who wins at Plateau de Beille will win the Tour—until 2011, the stage winner had won the Tour overall.

It was almost certain that such tradition would not continue for Vanendert, who attacked Cadel's group with 6.5 kilometres to go, caught and passed Frenchman Sandy Casar (Francaise des Jeux)—the last of a 20-strong break that formed after 5.5 kilometres—and was 20th overall at 12 minutes 6 seconds. 'Don't they say who wins here ... is the winner of the Tour? Maybe that means a breakaway is going to win', Cadel said, then adding more seriously: 'I don't know. It's always on consistency, being there every day. That's the way I approach it ... Maybe I'm wrong. I've come second twice, you know ...'

• • •

As the Tour progressed, it was noted by many observers that riders were showing more fatigue and strain than in past years. This raised the question of whether or not the 2011 Tour was a cleaner race, on the doping front, than in the past.

There are indications that, in general, the sport's being won on good training and talent. It is a good sign when riders are performing close together at the same level. Riders who, year after year, have consistently been at a good level are winning more often. You see less of those riders who do nothing much, jump out on one key day and then fade back into obscurity.

A cleaner race forces riders to ride more intelligently, simply because every move or effort made will tax vital energy more heavily. People also have to be more careful about staying in good position in the front of the group, and letting groups of riders go away. Despite the lack of 'phenomenal' performances, it is a better test of the better cyclists.

• • •

With every day of racing, Cadel was firming as the rider to beat—even Australian Stuart O'Grady, who was riding for Andy Schleck, thought so. As the Tour left the Pyrenees on stage 15 from Limoux to Montpellier, O'Grady said:

> Cadel looks a lot stronger, but the biggest thing I've noticed is that he looks calmer. He seems to have calmed his temperament, which is vital. The Tour is won not only mentally but physically.
>
> He seems to be much more relaxed. He is probably much more confident in himself. He has grown with experience. He is not out to prove anyone wrong. He is one of the strongest riders in the world and … he is probably favourite for the Tour.

Schleck's team manager, Brian Nygaard concurred:

More and more [Evans is the favourite]. We said it at the
beginning, to anyone who cares to listen, there are more
favourites than [just] us ... and Evans, if you see how he has
planned his season ... has perfectly timed it towards this race.
He looks like the man to beat.

Former Tour champion Stephen Roche, the Irish 1987
winner, was another who fancied Cadel's chances. He
doubted the Schleck brothers and criticised their strategy
in the Pyrenees, especially the commitment of their attacks
after all the work their team had done to set them up:

It was very disappointing having such fabulous terrain and not
much change in the general classification. Voeckler had a great
ride, a great ride—no discredit to his performance. But the big
guys didn't make use at all of the terrain. Andy kicked off in
the final 500 metres to Plateau de Beille to take 2 seconds out
of Contador—big deal. Why didn't he do it with 5 kilometres to
go? Why didn't Fränk counterattack? It's ridiculous at that level.
Evans was probably the most impressive. It was not for him to
attack. If the situation stays the way it is, Evans will win the Tour.

Asked how Cadel should race as the stage 19 time trial
loomed, Roche said: 'Do exactly what he is doing now—
maybe get some time back on Voeckler—and leave the
pressure on everybody else; and minimise any time loss to
Contador between now and the time trial.'

Italian Max Testa, BMC's head physician, said data showed that Cadel was as healthy as he had ever been this far into a Tour, when the body can break down and riders can lose weight, body fat and appetite to a dangerous degree and start suffering irregular sleep patterns:

Cadel has fast recovery; he is very healthy. He rarely gets sick. In 2010 with a broken elbow, he did the whole race to honour the world champion's jersey. From a medical view I would be happy to have nine riders like him. He is the perfect rider for this event. He is mentally very strong. He can separate and focus on the race and relax after. He can switch on and off like only big champions can.

Cadel, however, was still not getting ahead of himself. He remained focused on every day that passed without mishap, injury or major time loss on the key Pyrenean stages to Luz-Ardiden and Plateau de Beille. He did lose 20 seconds to Fränk Schleck on Luz-Ardiden, and 2 seconds to his brother Andy on Plateau de Beille but, if anything, those small gains by the brothers were small returns on the effort they and their teammates put in. And while the Schlecks were starting to show strain, Cadel was remarkably calm and at ease when under pressure.

But Voeckler was still a concern. As every day passed without any major change overall, the Frenchman's odds of an upset firmed. It was getting closer and closer to the goal in Paris, but Voeckler was also passing these days without losing time. Cadel was perhaps more wary of him than the others were, but when the race reached the Alps and Voeckler was still there, people were starting to worry.

Cadel had not forgotten Voeckler's form in his final Tour lead-up race, the Critérium du Dauphiné, in which the Australian placed second overall to Briton Bradley Wiggins (Sky) and Voeckler, who was third on the medium mountain stage to Les Gets, worked tirelessly for his French teammate Christophe Kerne. Kerne was sixth overall in the Dauphiné and set to lead the Europcar team until tendonitis in the knee saw him not start stage 6. Asked about Voeckler, Cadel said:

He was really good. Everyone was saying [before stage 14], 'he's going to lose yellow … he's going to lose yellow'. I am like, 'No way. I think he is going to go a few more days at least [in the Tour race leader's yellow jersey]'. He hangs in there every day and his [Europcar] team I would imagine are incredibly motivated here in France. Riding in yellow on Bastille Day for a French team …

Asked if it suited him that Voeckler was poised to wear the yellow jersey to the Alps and carry the pressure as the Tour tackled the flatter transition stages, Cadel laughed, then said, 'It wouldn't suit me if they have the jersey in the Champs Elysées. For now, we're still positioned well'.

It also suited the Luxembourg LeOpard team. For had Voeckler succumbed to the pace and the mountains and lost the jersey in the Pyrenees, as most expected, LeOpard would probably have had one of their riders in the Tour's yellow jersey, as Australian Stuart O'Grady (LeOpard) explained:

> Europcar are doing a really good job. Personally … that means I don't have to ride on the front. They [Europcar] get some good publicity out of it, and we have to look at the big picture. That's Paris. We will let them do their time and enjoy the moment. We will strike when necessary.

Contador was also still a concern for Cadel. Seventh overall at 4 minutes to Voeckler after the Pyrenees, Contador realised time was passing quickly and began testing his rivals with digs off the front—like a boxer with his jab. But the defensive racing grated on him; he said, 'This is a totally different kind of cycling to me; but for one reason or other, I'm not as strong as I want to be'. Had the Schlecks let the Tour slip from their grasps? Contador warned: 'Every day spent without dropping riders like Cadel Evans, it's getting harder for them to win.'

Cadel still braced himself for a massive attack like the one Contador produced on the climb to Verbier in the 2009 Tour, when the Spaniard blew the field apart and left all his rivals—Cadel included—gasping for air. The attacks never eventuated, but it's never wise to discount a rider like Contador. He's shown in the past what he can do when time-trialling and climbing, and with his mental strength. He has all the attributes and he has a record of results to prove his capabilities. He's always someone to be wary of.

LEAVING THE PYRENEES

Official overall standings (after 14 stages; 2448 kilometres)

1. Thomas Voeckler (Europcar) in 61 hours 4 minutes 10 seconds
2. Fränk Schleck (LeOpard) — 1 minute 49 seconds
3. Cadel Evans (BMC) — 2 minutes 6 seconds
4. Andy Schleck (LeOpard) — 2 minutes 15 seconds
5. Ivan Basso (Liquigas) — 3 minutes 16 seconds
6. Sammie Sánchez (Euskaltel-Euskadi) — 3 minutes 44 seconds
7. Alberto Contador (Saxo Bank-SunGard) — 4 minutes
8. Damiano Cunego (Lampre-ISD) — 4 minutes 1 second
9. Tom Danielson (Garmin-Cervélo) — 5 minutes 46 seconds
10. Kevin De Weert (QuickStep) — 6 minutes 18 seconds

When the Tour left the Pyrenees the battle lines for the overall race were clearer, with the official overall standings almost in line with Le Tour Virtual.

The principal changes reflected in Le Tour Virtual were that Voeckler was regarded as a serious contender after having held on to first place overall; and that Frenchman Jean-Christophe Péraud (Ag2r-La Mondiale)—officially 12th overall at 8 minutes 20 seconds to Voeckler—made it into the top 10.

12

FROM THE PYRENEES TO THE ALPS

Cadel Evans was not thinking only of the Tour de France during the rest day that fell on the eve of the 16th stage— 162 kilometres from Saint-Paul-Trois-Chateau in the Drôme to Gap at the foot of the Alps. The 16th stage was the second of two transition stages that took the Tour from the Pyrenees and towards the Alps after stage 15 from Limoux to Montpellier, and was won by British sprinter Mark Cavendish.

Cadel, still third overall at 2 minutes and 6 seconds to Thomas Voeckler, was not distracted, though. The riders were on tenterhooks with what awaited—three days in the Alps and a crucial 42-kilometre time trial in Grenoble. Cadel was perfectly placed and feeling strong, but the Mapei Day ride and dinner in Bormeo—in honour of his former trainer and mentor, Aldo Sassi—was on his mind.

Sassi, who set up the Mapei training centre that Cadel has often used, died in December 2010 after an operation for a brain tumour earlier that year. Mapei Day is a day where friends and supporters of Sassi ride to the famed summit of the Stelvio Pass—a 27-kilometre ascent of 48 hairpins that is a legendary climb in the Giro d'Italia. Due to his Tour commitments, Cadel could not attend the dinner or the ride, but he prepared a video that was presented to the dinner guests as encouragement for the next day, and as an homage to his still sadly missed mentor, Sassi.

Cadel was not the only rider in the Tour who had been close to Sassi and was racing as much for the trainer's honour as his own—one being Italian Ivan Basso, who had returned from a two-year suspension after admitting in 2007 his intent to dope. After winning the 2009 Giro in his comeback year, Basso pledged to Sassi that he would try and win the Tour for him. However, when the Tour left the Pyrenees the chances of Basso winning the 2011 Tour were looking slim. They were even slimmer by the time they neared the foot of the Alps—he was fifth overall at 3 minutes 16 seconds.

More telling was Basso's apparent struggle and wrestle with the bike. The general consensus was that the facial and shoulder injuries he sustained in a crash descending Mount Etna on a training ride had compromised his preparation more than most had realised. But despite that, in the 2011 Tour Basso was a discreet figure compared to the rider who had placed third in 2004 and second in 2005 to Armstrong, and who had won the 2010 Giro after coming back from his suspension. It appeared that he was also attracting far less attention from the media and fans.

Basso was considered a threat up until the Pyrenees arrived. He had had a setback with the crash in the training camp and, as usual when a rider is peaking a little late, he was progressing as the race went on. At Luz-Ardiden Basso was equal fourth with Cadel, and it seemed he was getting better—and for the right part of the race. Then, for some reason, his progression turned into a decline by the time the race reached the Alps. Along with his earlier time losses, it was not Basso's year.

However, in the 2011 Tour Cadel and Basso shared a unique bond in that they were both motivated by the legacy of Sassi, as they confirmed during the rest day that followed the 193-kilometre 15th stage from Limoux to Montpellier. Cadel, who spent the day at BMC's team hotel in the town of Valaurie, resting after a training ride, did not hold a press conference or conduct any interviews that day.

The decision to not make himself available for a press call upset some within the media corps. But when asked by a journalist in a text message what Mapei Day and Sassi meant to him at that point in time, when his focus was the Tour, Cadel replied:

> Aldo is always in my thoughts. Last year, riding the Tour with a broken arm was nothing compared to seeing his family suffer. He is the one man who has had faith in me through my entire road career. Only my legs worked harder than he did for me.

Basso, in an earlier interview with the *Sydney Morning Herald*, said, 'I speak a lot with his family to stay near to him. I feel him close to me. What I promised him was to give 100 per cent in the Tour'.

· · ·

Before the Tour, Cadel had broken down the route into four major sections: the run-up to the Pyrenees that included the team time trial; the Pyrenees; the Alps; and the final time trial in Grenoble. But with the Pyrenees behind him, Cadel's race for Tour victory was only really starting to hot up: getting past the Pyrenees was, for him, the half-way point of the Tour—but he still had two or three big mountain days and a time trial to go.

However, before those crucial last days arrived, there were still the ever-dangerous transitional stages to navigate from the Pyrenees to the foot of the Alps. Technically, they are not as challenging; but coming in the third week of the Tour, when riders start to weaken rapidly and concentration can waver due to accumulated fatigue, these stages can't be taken for granted. Only the riders with real talent perform at a high level in the third week. By the start of the week, everyone—mechanics, directors, journalists, the race organisers—is getting tired, but everyone's getting tired together.

It was also in the back of every Tour contender's mind that awaiting them all was that sting in the tail—those three Alpine stages and the Grenoble time trial. It had looked like there were 10 relatively easy days in the 2011 Tour, and then 10 days of really hard racing. Everything hinged on the second half—little bits were done in the first 10 days but, apart from Voeckler going in the stage 9 break, the big differences were all made in the second 10.

Unlike in the previous four of the six Tours Cadel started, he felt strong heading into the final week. In 2010 he was mentally fatigued from pushing himself with a broken elbow—even getting out of the hotel became frustrating.

Racing with that injury was also physically fatiguing—and of course the results weren't giving him any stimulation.

In 2009 Cadel was out of general classification, just riding to get training in. In 2007 and 2008 he was mentally exhausted from focusing and riding in position and fighting for position for two weeks. But because of what the team had done in 2011—they had delivered him there so well—Cadel was mentally much fresher and sharper going into the third week. And that was great, because that was when he was hoping to play his biggest moves.

Most riders lose weight during a grand tour, but Cadel's weight is reasonably consistent and rarely fluctuates from 68 kilograms, even going into the third week. Neither does he suffer the worrying drop in body fat that some experience—body-fat levels have been known to fall as low as 3 per cent in some riders, with their skin resembling a road map because their veins are visible. If a rider's body is not breaking down and losing muscle, it means their recovery is going well. The times Cadel has lost body weight during the grand tours—in the 2002 Giro d'Italia, for example—have been when he's come unstuck in the second half of the race.

After a few years of racing, riders learn what is right for themselves—and everyone is different. Leaner is not necessarily better. Of course it's lighter—better for climbing and in hot weather—but it can also mean less resistance to illness, compromised recovery, and loss of muscle and therefore strength.

It's vital in the third week of the Tour that riders maintain their fluid and food intake, even if appetites fall, which can happen—especially when the race is in the hotter and more humid climes of southern France, or in the desolate rural environs of the Massif Central, through which many transition stages traditionally pass.

Once a rider starts to drink more than 2 litres an hour in a six-hour stage, it becomes a lot of work for their stomach. It is all part of the training and adaptation the body goes through to become a grand tour rider.

Professional bike riders view food as fuel, but maintaining the right calorie intake does take a conscious effort. If a rider has an appetite, it's a sign of good form—when the motor is going, so is the metabolism. A loss of appetite is a bad sign.

Cadel enjoys good food, but, like most riders, he eats simply on the Tour: plain pasta, plain rice, vegetables and meat, chicken or fish. As long as it is fresh and well prepared, it satisfies his appetite and nutritional requirements.

Elite riders are aware of what they need—certain fuel and vitamins and minerals and so on, but psychological satisfaction is also important. Allowing for personal food preferences is one way to avoid eating becoming a chore. In the Tour there are plenty of demands and stresses, and an enjoyable meal at the start or end of another torturous day in the saddle can boost morale.

Many teams have their own chef. At BMC the chef is Peter Cambre, who Cadel regularly asks for tailor-made meals that suit his palate.

Now and then the team asks for something special, like pancakes for breakfast. It will always have good carbohydrates and provide what the riders need for fuel and recovery, but with something a little extra to add a little enjoyment, whether it's sauce or topping or dessert. But it takes energy to digest food, and considering the large energy expenditure and required calorie uptake, keeping food choices a bit simpler does help.

• • •

Cadel needed every ounce of energy by the time the Tour reached the foot of the Alps on stage 16 to Gap and entered the mountain range on stage 17 from Gap to Pinerolo in Italy—two stages that were terrific precursors to the action that unfolded in the three days before the finish in Paris. The stages did not determine the fate of any overall contender, but revealed the likely game plan they would employ in the days ahead.

Contador revealed his intent with five attacks on the last climb on the 16th stage, the 9-kilometre-long Col de Manse that began on the outskirts of Gap and took the riders back out to the countryside before dropping into the city centre under torrents of rain to the finish. Hushovd (Garmin-Cervélo) outsprinted Norway's Edvald Boasson Hagen (Sky) and Canadian Ryder Hesjedal (Garmin-Cervélo) to win the stage.

The stage leaders did not figure in the overall classification and so were not cause for concern. But Cadel sensed that Contador would attack on the last climb before the finish, and he knew that it was imperative to be in the right place if he was to follow. Again, his teammates came to the fore.

It was a struggle for the riders behind to get in position, but Cadel was second wheel going through Gap at the start of the climb. He even had time to take off his jacket and give it to a teammate. The team put him in an excellent position and Cadel was able to finish it off.

Contador led over the top of the Col de Manse with Spaniard Sammie Sánchez (Euskaltel-Euskadi), a renowned descender. But thanks to his position, Cadel was able to set off in pursuit and then catch and attack Sánchez to finish three seconds clear of him and Contador, who finished 13th and 12th on the stage respectively. Cadel's time gain—even if only seconds—was a demonstration of the team's capabilities. Taking time when people weren't expecting them to make or do anything because the break was away was a stamp of authority over Contador and the race.

• • •

The success that came with stage 16 to Gap was no cause for Cadel to relax: the days ahead would determine the outcome of the Tour. Cadel tapped into his mountain-biking skills for these days, especially when he chased Contador into Gap. It was only a small time-gap to Contador and Sánchez, but it started to be a significant gap for Basso and Andy Schleck: Cadel's 11th place to Hushovd at 4 minutes 23 seconds saw him gain 3 seconds on Contador; 21 seconds on Fränk Schleck and 13 others, including Voeckler; 54 seconds on

Basso; and 2 minutes 3 seconds on Andy Schleck. Cadel's chase was ignited by BMC team sports director John Lelangue's order, 'it's time to go' over the race radio.

It wasn't a stage where Contador could make a big difference, but by that time in the Tour he had to attack whenever he could. Cadel was able to follow him and react, and it put him in a great position. The descent was quite narrow and windy, and the bad weather made it even more intimidating, but Cadel's experience in the wet and in mountains was an advantage. A number of observers felt he was taking risks in the rain; general classification riders can't afford to take risks, but Cadel was certainly staying within his limits. It was a bad road but, having been a mountain biker, he has adapted to bad roads in wet conditions and on tight corners—and the top-notch Continental tyres he was using perform exceptionally well in wet weather.

Cadel doesn't use his descending prowess to force rivals out of the race, as many felt the great Belgian rider Eddy Merckx did in the 1971 Tour in the Pyrenees. While descending the Col de Menté at breakneck speed with race leader Luis Ocana right on his wheel, Merckx lost control in a downpour and skidded into a wall. Ocana was unable to avoid him and crashed as well. While Merckx quickly remounted and raced off, Ocana's misfortune ended his Tour—he was taken to hospital in Saint-Gaudens, surrendering his overall race lead.

While Merckx refused to wear the yellow jersey he won through Ocana's absence the next day, the incident led many to question whether Merckx had crossed the line into poor sportsmanship by setting the formidable pace on the descent.

There seem to have been more narrow and 'technical' descents in the last few Tours, and many believe that Tour organisers must shoulder responsibility for including descents so close to stage finishes like those to Gap and to Pinerolo in Italy the next day. Having the bad luck to get a puncture caused by a bad road is not something a rider can prepare for.

Still, cyclists are there to race, and bad luck can happen anywhere—uphill, downhill and on the flat. In the 2008 Tour Cadel had the misfortune to crash on stage 9 after Spanish rider Gorka Verdugo (Euskaltel-Euskadi) crashed in front of him. Verdugo hadn't realised the turn was so sharp, so he turned abruptly at the wrong moment, and dropped it. It wasn't a dangerous descent—not even a dangerous turn—but it cost Cadel a lot.

Cadel's strong finish at Gap confirmed what many suspected: that he was finishing the Tour stronger than Sánchez and Contador. It was a very good sign for the BMC team. Holding off Sánchez and Contador on the flat kilometres to the line was a good indication for the upcoming time trial. They were just behind Cadel; he didn't look back, but he was getting time checks every few seconds over the radio. His teammates were also receiving the same information, to their delight, some kilometres behind him:

I wasn't expecting so much [activity] on the climb. I was more prepared for things on the downhill, actually, because it's a little bit dangerous and so on. I got in front alone and followed the moves. George [Hincapie] and Burgy [Burghardt] got me in the right position, right at the bottom of the last climb. I just had to play my cards as they came out. It's still a bit of a blur right now … it was a good little move and a good day.

It reflected his confidence, too, that when Contador launched his attacks on the climb, his pursuit was not panicked, but in assured control of what was unfolding:

There [were] still 21 or 22 kilometres to go … It was not like he was going to go from there alone normally … so I just took my time, looked around and saw what was going on. You have to be really careful in these [stages] where you are so close on the GC. As we saw at Plateau de Beille and Luz-Ardiden [with it] being such close racing, it's the guys coming [from] behind [that] can be the danger.

Andy Schleck was clearly down:

It was a dangerous finish. I didn't feel super on the climb, when [Contador] attacked. I rode badly downhill, I had to unclip on the first corner and was gapped 150 metres. I couldn't coast to the bottom.

However, he didn't read too much into the impact of his time loss:

I don't think it means anything, I am confident and my form is good. I showed it and I am going to show it again. I will keep my head up for the next days. I am pretty disappointed, but if this [is] what people want to see, a race decided on a downhill ... I think the [route] was badly chosen today. We don't want to see riders crashing or taking risks. Everyone has families at home. A finish like this should not be allowed.

Another consequence, according to BMC team president Jim Ochowicz, was that Contador, with his obvious intent to attack in the Tour's final stages, emerged as a possible ally for Cadel—assuming that Cadel could follow his planned moves and then possibly counterattack, as he did into Gap. After the stage, Ochowicz said: 'Contador wants to win the Tour and has to do something to make that happen. One of them was what he just did.' And, Ochowicz added, by not following Contador and Evans, the Schlecks showed they were vulnerable.

The idea of an alliance between Contador and Cadel would not have been considered possible previously, given the competitive history between the two riders and the fact that the Spaniard was the defending champion. It was to Contador that Cadel placed second at only 23 seconds in the 2007 Tour. But in 2009 Contador rode to help Alejandro Valverde win the Critérium du Dauphiné stage race in France, even though the two Spaniards were on different teams.

By the time the 2011 Tour was in the Alps, the prospect of an allegiance between Cadel and Contador had become very real—especially on stage 18 to Galibier Serre-Chevalier.

Contador and Cadel are normally competing against each other in races, whether it's at the Tour du Pays Basque, the

Dauphiné or the Tour de France. They have never actually had many opportunities to talk in a normal, relaxed environment, but Cadel is aware that Contador's ex-teammates and people who know him all have a tremendous amount of respect for him as a person; they praise his human qualities, and depict him as being quite modest and simple. He still lives with his family in the village where he was born, enjoys good food and wine and the company of his family. He also just happens to be one of the hardest bike riders to beat at the Tour—and in any of the hilly, hard races that Cadel is suited to.

• • •

As Cadel recovered in the BMC team bus after his efforts at Gap, he was unaware that standing outside in the crowd was Phil Anderson, the first Australian ever to wear the Tour's yellow jersey, in 1981; he finished five times in the top 10 overall, and took two fifth places. Anderson, who retired in 1994 after a career that included two Tour stage wins and numerous other victories, is considered the modern-day pioneer in Australia's journey towards becoming a major cycling nation. Anderson resumed the journey that fellow Victorians Don Kirkham and Iddo 'Snowy' Munro began in 1914 as the first Australians to race in the Tour—a feat that inspired the great Sir Hubert Opperman to race it in 1928, when he placed 18th overall, and in 1931, when he placed 12th.

It was fitting that, 30 years after his first spell in the yellow jersey, Anderson was there as Evans edged towards becoming the first Australian Tour winner. It would go down as one of the greatest achievements by an Australian sports star, but Anderson's place in history set the mark.

Not that Anderson was worried about being eclipsed in history. He told the media:

> It's bloody exciting for cycling in Australia. It's bloody huge. Since Mûr de Bretagne you can see he is so much on top of the others. He's ridden a better race and looks stronger than in past years.

Cadel only learned about Anderson's presence that day in Gap several months after the Tour, and he was genuinely taken with Anderson's excitement for him. He started watching the Tour as a 14 year old in the 1990s, when Miguel Indurain started his winning streak. Indurain was the man Cadel admired most, but Anderson was the one he was cheering for.

•   •   •

The steep 6.7 kilometre–long climb up the Côte de Pramartino, to the stage 17 finish in Pinerolo, is on sinewy, narrow roads and was destined to provoke a scramble for position near the front—to be ready for any attack or to be well placed near any move to respond to it. Positioning at the start of the second-category climb was vital because of the challenge that would face riders caught at the back of the congested roadway. And because of the twists and turns, any rider up front who broke away could quickly find himself out of the peloton's sight and on course for a win. But of more concern was the descent into Pinerolo. The twisting, narrow roads and broken cover of branches from the surrounding forest created blinding flashes of evening sunlight—perfect crash conditions.

The descent into Pinerolo was as frenetic as expected. Cadel was again one of the principal beneficiaries, moving into second place overall at 1 minute 18 seconds to Voeckler, who was extremely lucky to avoid disaster on the descent to the finish; he misjudged a corner and rode into a car park while following an attack by Contador and Sánchez.

Cadel always had a sense of trepidation about the stage 17 finish into Pinerolo, and for that reason he and teammate Ivan Santaromita drove there after finishing the Tour de Romandie to conduct a reconnaissance of the final climb and descent.

It was difficult to believe that the Tour was going to run on this road—the publicity caravan wasn't even able to fit through. Cadel and Santaromita were so convinced that they had misunderstood the course that when it came to racing in the stage, they were shocked to discover it was the right road. They had thought the route would take the main road, rather than the narrow turn-off.

However, fortune was on Cadel's side. Teammate George Hincapie had led Cadel to an ideal position at the foot of the climb where he was ready to respond to the unexpected route direction—although his acceleration and jostling for position onto Hincapie's wheel did catch another teammate, Manuel Quinziato, out.

They were approaching a roundabout and Cadel realised he had to move up. When he went to go up on the side he found an enormous hole, jumped right over it, got on the wheel and sneaked into the right position—which took Quinziato, who was behind Cadel, by surprise.

Cadel got on Hincapie's wheel and came into the bottom corner. Both of his tyres slid into a right-hand turn, and Hincapie dropped him off right in the front.

Santaromita went to go around Cadel on the climb, and as he went to take him up in the wind he realised he couldn't go faster. Coming at about the time Contador had attacked for the first of two times on the climb with Schleck chasing, Cadel found himself blocked by Santaromita. However, Cadel was able to get around his Italian teammate before catching up with Contador and Schleck. But then, as Cadel was about to try and place himself in front of Contador and Schleck before going over the top of the climb, someone he couldn't see attacked and he hesitated slightly—which was a mistake: they were approaching a very tight, narrow stretch of road, which was in deep shadow, making it difficult for many riders to see. In a minute or so the riders emerged from the shadow and were blinded by the light.

Cadel was further back than he wanted to be. And he realised Contador and now Sánchez were off the front. On the descent Voeckler was chasing the Spaniards with a vengeance, determined to defend the yellow jersey and, to the shock of Cadel, who was behind him, almost crashed twice as he rode off course. Meanwhile, as Contador and Sánchez continued racing towards the finish, Edvald Boasson Hagen (Sky) was in the throes of solo chase, and soon caught and counterattacked the pair to win the stage. In the aftermath, Cadel, who also caught Contador and Sánchez entering the finishing straight, was still second overall, but at 1 minute 18 seconds to Voeckler who lost 27 seconds to him, Contador, the Schlecks and Sánchez.

Later, Cadel lamented to reporters the dangers of the final descent:

It was a bit different, dryer and more corners, and more shadowy … but I didn't want to take any risk. Voeckler ran off the road twice in front of me. It makes you take things a bit more cautiously. It doesn't inspire you to go cutting around and taking risks. So they had a gap and that was sort of opened up by the guys behind and fortunately we closed it down on the flat there. I've got a good advantage over Alberto now, but he has shown what he can do when he's at his top.

Ultimately you would want to go into the final time trial with a five- to 10-minute [lead]. Unfortunately, I don't think that's going to happen.

Cadel and the BMC team knew that fireworks awaited them in the Alps. But, as John Lelangue said, they were ready for the fight:

We are pretty good at this. This is his kind of racing. He is the best in this scenario. It's an ideal situation to be in this position at the end of the Tour.

We've answered all the attacks. We know we can do it and are confident because we have [after 17 stages] eight teammates [to support Cadel].

And Cadel, despite the pressure building on every contender, was clearly embracing the contest and the increasing outside interest in it. 'It's a very closely raced Tour and the contenders are very closely matched … I have really enjoyed it', he was reported as saying. 'Everyone here is really looking after one another and that makes difficult moments that little bit easier'. Unlike in 2009, he was even accepting of his billing as the favourite to win the Tour. 'I think it's something that you kind of earn and I feel like I am earning it', Cadel said. 'I'll say. I'm actually enjoying it.'

• • •

The finish in Pinerolo was chaotic. Team buses were parked in various pockets around the finish area—but BMC's bus was not there. Half the staff hadn't been able to get there in time because the roads were blocked; it was a very disorganised afternoon, and the team's recovery process wasn't as smooth as they were used to.

Instead of recovering in the air-conditioned luxury of the 15-metre BMC bus, Cadel, who finished 20th at 4 minutes 26 seconds to Boasson Hagen, recovered in the tight, hot and humid confines of a van.

Cadel spoke briefly to media outside, but was keen for privacy after a tense and tough finish. And with what was to come in the next three days—two backbreaking stages in the Alps and the Grenoble time trial, and some long transfers—BMC team management announced that after a one-on-one interview with the *Sydney Morning Herald* and SBS Television that night, a media blackout on access to Cadel would be enforced.

It was almost 8.30 pm by the time Cadel had had his nightly massage from David Bombeke, fulfilled his final media commitments before the shutdown, and farewelled his wife, Chiara, and dog, Molly, for the last time before the finish in Paris. He was exhausted.

13

THE GREAT PURSUIT

Many who had studied the route and calibre of riders in contention believed victory in the 2011 Tour de France would be determined by stages 18 and 19 in the Alps and the stage 20 time trial in Grenoble. But no-one tipped the drama that would unfold in the three stages. The 18th stage from Pinerolo to Galibier Serre-Chevalier confirmed that the Tour would not be decided by any one stage, but as a consequence of what happened in each of those three stages—each affected how the next was raced.

By stage 18, most felt that Andy Schleck had to act but, given his aggressive racing in the previous two stages, Alberto Contador was still very much a threat. There was a chance he would attack on L'Alpe d'Huez, but it seemed more likely that the longer stage to Galibier, with its longer climbs, was Contador's comeback opportunity. Stage 18 was the first big climb—it was just getting going, but it was also wearing all the riders down.

Cadel knew the route well. He had ridden over parts of it in a training camp, from the 17-kilometre descent of the Col d'Izoard to the 23-kilometre ascent of the Galibier from the south, to the ski station of Serre-Chevalier in a headwind—including many passages through Briançon.

But racing on the route is far different to training on it; and not just because of the tactics rival riders may want to employ or not employ. The crowds and their cars and campervans also affect conditions for riders: not just in terms of support, but because they block the wind. This is something riders take into consideration when preparing for the Tour, but can only ever really respond to when the big day arrives.

Whether there's a headwind, tailwind or sidewind doesn't make that big a difference except when there's a stretch of about 40 kilometres and at least 20 riders are exposed to the wind. The route comes out of Briançon and starts up the valley, and from the 165-kilometre mark to the 191-kilometre mark—at the Col du Lautaret when the course turns onto the Galibier climb with 8.5 kilometres to go—the headwind does make a difference.

Schleck or Contador had to launch some offensive to keep their Tour hopes alive, so it was imperative Cadel had riders to help him. It was going to be one of the biggest days of the Tour. Two hundred kilometres is a big stage, and the big climbs to high altitude were going to put everyone on their limit. But what no-one could foresee was that this day, of all days, would be the BMC team's worst day.

Two of Cadel's teammates, Marcus Burghardt and Brent Bookwalter, went with an early attack to ensure they were up front and able to drop back to help Cadel in the likelihood they would be caught and that he would need assistance.

As they descended the Col d'Izoard, Bookwalter dropped back. He was struggling and felt it was better to come back and be useful rather than stay there and get dropped. But it wasn't just Bookwalter who was struggling: Hincapie, Schär and Quinziato had all let Cadel know they were having an off day, and Santaromita had a knee injury. Every other day of the Tour the team was firing on all cylinders, but from early in the stage it was clear this was going to be a tough day for the BMC team. There was still hope, though: often a rider feels bad at the start, but finishes racing strongly.

• • •

The pace on the Col d'Agnel was irregular until Bookwalter got into the first breakaway, whose escape helped to settle the pace behind them. But on the approach to the Col d'Izoard it picked up again under the steam of Andy Schleck's LeOpard teammates—Australian Stuart O'Grady and German Jens Voigt, who rode on the front at a fierce tempo. It looked like they were going to attack, but it was still unclear which card LeOpard would deal—Andy Schleck, or Fränk. Cadel was right with Andy when he went.

And when Andy did break free and attack from the right of the group, Cadel's first thought was to let him go, knowing that up front there was still the breakaway group, including Bookwalter. But then the stage kicked up several gears: LeOpard went across and the group formed in front—and Bookwalter got caught.

Bookwalter re-joined Cadel's group and rode at a good tempo all the way up the Col d'Izoard—so good a tempo that a struggling Hincapie was unable to hold on. BMC needed to keep the gap within range, but they knew the headwind was coming so decided to let Andy go and expend his energy. But the group in front took more time on the descent than Cadel expected.

Morabito came up and rode all the way into Briançon, through Briançon and then started up the valley. Then Amaël Moinard recovered, came back and rode with what he had left. But then everyone else in the group started to panic, and Euskaltel-Euskadi came in with four or five riders.

Cadel was going to need help to bring Schleck back: if there was no chase by this point it was possible his Tour hopes could be squandered. He had expected to take back some time on the descent, hit the valley and then take back even more time; instead, he kept losing time, and everyone was exhausted.

Even worse was that the speed was too fast and Cadel's group began to splinter, two victims being Cadel's teammates Morabito and Moinard. Up front, Andy Schleck, who had two teammates—Maxime Monfort and Joost Posthuma—in another breakaway group further up the road and ready to drop back and help their leader if needed, extended his lead as he rode down the valley into a headwind towards the final climb. At La Salles-les-Alpes, with 28 kilometres to go, it seemed the Tour was escaping.

Cadel's instinct was to look around the group and see which of the other leaders who were losing time had teammates with them who could help in the chase. Ivan Basso was not losing places on general classification, so he didn't really need to help. Damiano Cunego didn't have any teammates. Sylwester

Szmyd, who was one of Basso's best mountain domestiques at the Dauphiné in 2010, was struggling himself.

Cadel asked Voeckler to ride, but Voeckler refused. In hindsight, this was most likely a mistake on his part. If he had co-operated (and he certainly could have—he had a teammate who was climbing very well and went on to win the next stage) he may have made it onto the final podium.

Cadel was perplexed to say the least:

When Voeckler and his team stopped riding and he has the yellow [jersey], it was a bit bizarre and strange. They've been riding a lot all week, but he had a teammate in the end, too. They looked at me to do the work, but I was alone, too.

Bike racing is a battle of wits, and it is difficult to know for sure if a rider is bluffing when they say they are having a bad day or are unable to ride in a collaborative effort for a common cause. Some riders, like Basso, are in general quite generous with their help—when he sees someone in trouble he'll help them when he can. Cunego collaborated with Cadel when he rode in to Pinerolo. But on stage 18 Voeckler was very happy where he was—and if he'd wanted to help someone, it's unlikely it was going to be Cadel.

But there was a risk in spending time trying to garner support for a chase—the longer Cadel spent, the more time Schleck had to extend his lead. People often talk about what riders discuss and how they collaborate, but letting up riding for 10 or 20 seconds in a headwind costs time—and there's no guarantee that any cooperation will eventuate.

Cadel couldn't afford to lose time, but there wasn't an option: there were riders who could come back and help, but by then it would be well and truly over.

Then, without warning and shortly before Cadel had reached the last 10 kilometres of the stage, Contador surprised Cadel by approaching him and saying that they needed to ride. They both started to ride; Contador took one or two turns quite hard, but then Cadel went on to the front, and later the tempo he set to save his Tour would prove too much for Contador to follow.

One of the novelties of this stage finish was that at an altitude of 2600 metres, it was the highest ever finish in the Tour. The altitude increased with every pedal stroke, but was of no concern to Cadel—he and his team were prepared for it, as were most riders.

At high altitude the body gets less oxygen and so is less able to generate power. At a certain heart rate your power will be less because of the lower oxygen content in the air, unless you're very well adapted. By that stage of the race it was not a case of the better riders coming more prepared. They'd all been racing and doing the same workload for 18 days.

Cadel's pursuit was not just a show of his physical prowess. It was also a psychological triumph for which he drew on his 20 years of experience. Cadel had the legs to ride tempo for 10 kilometres, but it was also vital he remain calm and gauge his energy output—which was made easier by the encouragement of John Lelangue via radio.

• • •

The timing of Cadel's chase was calculated; he waited until he got to an area that was a little bit more covered. It was still a big group with little co-operation, and he didn't want to ride into a headwind with the group behind him. They approached a tunnel that was slightly protected at the bottom—and Cadel started to ride. He realised no-one was going to give him any help.

Voeckler, Contador, Basso and his Liquigas teammates were all there, but no-one wanted to work—including Basso's teammate Sylwester Szmyd, who was strong one or two days before. By that point Cadel had begun his chase, and his only remaining hope for support was Contador. But he did not—or could not—help. The Spaniard was cooked.

Where they emerged from the tunnel the road goes left. There was a crosswind, so Cadel started riding on the left to force everyone into the wind, and then started riding at a tempo he could maintain—but with a bit in reserve to call on whenever other riders went on the attack.

When Cadel reached the Col du Lautaret, part of the Galibier, after 14 kilometres of climbing and still in front and doing all the work, it was a critical point: had he not acted, he could easily have lost the Tour.

Cadel continued riding. And as John Lelangue saw the selection from behind in the car and the groups of riders getting dropped—he began feeling very optimistic. At 5 kilometres to go he was on the radio telling Cadel which riders had been dropped, that the group was 12 strong, nine strong ... that Cunego was struggling. And then that Contador was struggling.

Cadel was at a good level and riding hard, but still keeping a bit in reserve and making surges he could control. Ideally, Cadel would have made lots of surges and accelerations and dropped all the riders, but that could also have put him in trouble. He rode at a regular tempo, constantly winding it up.

As Cadel continued his pursuit of Andy Schleck he got the news, over race radio, that Contador had been dropped. There was quite possibly no news that could have been more encouraging to Cadel on the climb into a headwind. He just kept riding.

Undoubtedly Cadel wanted to catch Andy and win the stage, but he also had to be realistic about bringing the time gap below the 2-minute barrier first. Another concern was Fränk Schleck, who was consistently there on the wheel.

Observers had expected Fränk to start attacking with about 3 kilometres to go. He did attack, but far later than expected—on the last left-hand corner with 300 metres to go. The Luxembourger was either fatigued by his effort at the front, or he lacked the confidence to go earlier; Cadel had managed to put him in a fair bit of difficulty, and that was promising for the future. Fränk gained 1 or 2 seconds, which of course Cadel would not have wanted to lose, but he had just ridden an almost uninterrupted 9.5 kilometres at the front to the end of the stage. There was almost a sprint, but Cadel didn't have the legs. It is one thing to ride up a hill fast, but to do it in the third week of the Tour, on the last mountain of the stage, and in high altitude is quite another.

Cadel's last kilometre was sensational. He peeled back another 45 seconds in that stretch, which finished with a steep 9 per cent–plus gradient pitch on the final corner, and which he tackled with near perfection. The same could be said of Andy Schleck, whose cadence stalled as he fought to push out his effort to the end before claiming a nonetheless impressive stage win.

The day's drama was widely seen as a measure of Cadel's ability to remain calm when under pressure. The real test of someone is when they're really on the limit. Cadel had been on the limit many times before, and he showed he was committed to pushing through. He also had the legs pull it off—and was able to put everyone else on the limit so that they couldn't mount a significant attack.

It was some time after the stage that Cadel managed to catch up with his teammates at the hotel. While they all finished the stage after Cadel, they didn't lose time fulfilling media commitments and were able to quickly grab a jacket and ride back down the mountain. Because of media and other obligations, and concern that he might catch a cold this late in the Tour by riding in the chill of late afternoon when he was still sweating, Cadel travelled in a car driven by John Lelangue.

As Cadel's car began its journey down through the traffic, his teammates stopped as they passed to tell him, 'Great job, great job'. They had monitored the progress of his chase through their radios while they were still racing, and had sensed he was on a truly great ride that would save his Tour.

Brent Bookwalter, who lost contact with Cadel on the Col d'Izoard, couldn't pick up race radio, but he saw a giant television screen on a switchback with about 6 kilometres to go:

I was cross-eyed trying to get to the finish. I was totally
miserable, maybe the most miserable I had been the whole
Tour. Then I saw Cadel on the front ripping this group to
shreds. I was like, 'He's doing it!'

George Hincapie, on the way to the stage start the next
day, said, 'Man, you are going to win this Tour'. Recalling
Cadel's chase, Hincapie says:

He may not be as physiologically good as Contador or Lance
Armstrong, but he can put himself in the hurt locker more
than anybody in the world.

• • •

At 6.30 pm Cadel finally arrived at the BMC team hotel …
and by then the exhaustion from such a tough marathon
stage, and the long transfer from the finish to the hotel, had
hit. David Bombeke, Cadel's personal osteopath, could see
his fatigue immediately and allowed Cadel some space and
time before getting him onto the massage table.

Timing is never perfect on the Tour. Logistically and
behind the scenes it can be fatiguing. When riders have
raced 6 or 7 hours and are then stuck in traffic for 2 hours,
they want a good night's sleep and a long massage. Things
can quickly get out of sync, and the flow-on effects can be
almost unbearable—the last thing riders need is to arrive
late for dinner and find the food they need is not available.
Or that they have to wait an hour before being served.

It is for that reason that BMC, like many teams, employs a personal chef. Peter Cambre is a Belgian who used to work on Cadel's former team, Lotto, but whose background is in the music industry, in which he worked as a chef for the American singer Bruce Springsteen.

Cadel doesn't rush his meals. As important as they are for refuelling, there is also the mental release of relaxing at a dinner table with teammates. After dinner he listens to music, Bob Dylan and Bruce Springsteen being two favourites; but his taste is not shared by his teammates. Not that they need worry—he doesn't have energy to set up speakers when he gets to his room, so he always takes earphones.

One thing a lot of the top riders have in common is they're very well organised. Their suitcases are neat and orderly, and contain only what they need and nothing more. They know exactly where everything is—they don't waste time getting things out, and they keep personal things to a minimum.

Some riders spend every minute possible recovering—to the point of sitting on their beds with their mobile phone, Blackberry, race book and recovery drink around them, legs up, not moving until they have to go to massage or dinner. Cadel doesn't usually go to such extremes—he'll move around a bit, listen to music or read a book. Sometimes he goes for a short walk after dinner, or will have a coffee with his teammates and compromise a bit of sleep and recovery time to think and talk about something other than the Tour.

•　•　•

Cadel's initiative on the ascent to Galibier Serre-Chevalier saved his Tour. He put about 20 years' racing experience to use that day. Not just the training, the physiology and the capacity to push, but his race judgement and ability to stay calm amongst it all.

After one of the most dogged and impressive chases seen by a Tour contender to save their Tour dreams, Cadel was on the cusp of true greatness. Although adding to the drama of a sensational Tour, the stage to Galibier Serre-Chevalier left many questions.

Could Andy Schleck and Cadel recover overnight for the next major battle on the road to l'Alpe d'Huez? Would Fränk Schleck be the next LeOpard grenade to be thrown and explode? Would Voeckler, who had said he had zero chance of winning the Tour a few days earlier, do the supposedly impossible—once again—and hang on to his yellow jersey? What did Contador have left in his legs? Did he have that one Tour-winning attack in him? Amid all the questions, one thing was sure: it had been a long time since the Tour had been so open for so many with only three days to go.

Going into the 109-kilometre stage 19 from Modane to the summit of l'Alpe d'Huez, Cadel was fourth overall at 1 minute 12 seconds to Voeckler, after finishing third on the stage at 2 minutes 15 seconds.

Andy Schleck was second overall at 15 seconds; and his brother Fränk, having outsprinted Cadel for second place on the stage at 2 minutes 7 seconds to his younger brother, was third overall at 1 minute 8 seconds.

14

BATTLE ON THE L'ALPE D'HUEZ

Cadel Evans knew there was no escape from the last-gasp bid by his main rivals still hoping to surpass him in the overall classification on the 109.5-kilometre 19th stage from Modane to l'Alpe d'Huez. The stage was destined to be explosive because of its relative shortness and the inclusion of three iconic climbs: the ascent of 16.7 kilometre–long Col du Télégraphe; the northern ascent of the 18.1-kilometre Col du Galibier, which the Tour had climbed the day before from the opposite face; and the 13.8-kilometre l'Alpe d'Huez. And with Cadel so well suited to the 20th stage—a 42.5-kilometre time trial in Grenoble—this was the last opportunity for most rivals to shore up any overall time advantage before the 3430-kilometre Tour finished on the Champs Elysées in Paris two days later.

The northern passage of the Galibier is technically harder than the southern, depending on how it is raced and the conditions that prevail, and with it coming before the final climb to l'Alpe d'Huez, its importance carried extra weight. There are also three stretches of the climb, including the last kilometre, that ascend at almost 10 per cent. But Cadel approached the Col du Télégraphe and the Galibier as one massive 34-kilometre ascent, interrupted by a 6-kilometre descent that is so fast it allows only for a quick drink. The downhill stage start from Modane to the foot of the Col du Télégraphe ensured an electric start to the climb.

Because it was a downhill start, there was reason to be wary of crashes. Everyone was exhausted from the day before and concentration was waning. Some of the big roads are typically littered with rocks and other debris, and there was a good chance of getting a puncture.

Despite his knowledge of the route, Cadel misjudged his positioning on the Col du Télégraphe, about 6 kilometres into the entire 34-kilometre climb to the Galibier.

He was too far back. All of a sudden everyone started to panic, and Contador hit out almost immediately. Cadel came back to the front and went with Voeckler across to the break where Andy Schleck was already away. Pierre Rolland and Sánchez joined soon after.

At the bottom of the Galibier, just after the descent from the Télégraphe, Cadel was with Contador, Schleck, Sánchez, Cunego, Voeckler and Rolland when he suddenly dropped off the pace. He rode out of the saddle, dancing on the pedals to get some momentum back. Observers wondered what had happened. Cadel later said that he felt his brakes were rubbing on the bike frame.

He continued to ride out of the saddle, until he looked down and saw that his rear wheel appeared to have moved within the frame. He continued to test it but could still feel it touching and opted to stop, even though all groups were spread out on the climb and the team cars were nowhere to be seen. Cadel undid the quick-release and made sure it was straight, then did it up and felt it was still a bit loose. He tried once more, then got back on the saddle and re-joined Contador's group; it became loose again, prompting him to undo and tighten it up one more time—but it was still rubbing. As soon as the BMC team car arrived he changed bikes, and then he was back up racing.

Some observers suspected that the bike frame had suffered structural damage, and those suspicions quickly filtered throughout the Tour entourage, but it appears that the problem was with the rear lightweight quick-release. All mechanics—Cadel's personal mechanic Antonio Biron included—are always focused on ensuring that bikes are right at the weight limit for individual riders. Cadel's bike ran 50 grams over the weight limit. Fifty grams may not make a difference, but BMC wanted lighter-weight quick-releases used for the mountain stages.

Cadel recalled the incident to reporters later, saying:

> I was sitting well but I was feeling pretty average, but I think, 'There's something wrong with my rear wheel' that was slowing me down a bit. When there was an acceleration it put me over the limit, which seemed bit strange. [The breaks] were rubbing on the frame, I think. It takes a fair bit of wasted energy. I wasn't sure about it, but it felt like it and for that reason I changed bikes.

In hindsight the incident served as a lesson to all that having the lightest equipment does not necessarily make for the best bike. For most riders, comfort and reliability come before lightness and performance—it's often better to go on the heavy side with a reliable item.

Today there are standards in the wheel industry, and the current rules demand a minimum bike weight of 6.8 kilograms, but years ago people would try and get their bikes down to 5.5 kilograms. The safety issues surrounding equipment standards are considerable: if someone's front wheel explodes in the middle of the peloton due to faulty material, it can cause a serious accident.

Cadel's fate was not thrown into danger when he had his mechanical problem on the Galibier—even though everyone who watched thought otherwise. Once again, a key figure in keeping the calm was Cadel's teammate George Hincapie who, when his group caught him as had been the plan, told him to 'sit up'. Meanwhile, Hincapie had also told the other BMC riders in the group to go harder at the front; that way, Cadel would be able to conserve more energy and go harder later.

But hearts were still in throats for everyone watching, as they feared Cadel was on the cusp of another race-costing disaster that would dog his career. He had his crashes in 2009 and 2010; and few had forgotten the slow rear-wheel change he'd had after puncturing on the second-last climb in the 13th stage of the 2009 Vuelta a España, when he'd been placed third overall and was on the cusp of taking the overall lead. Fortunately in this case, the mechanical problem happened early enough in the race that Cadel and the team were able to manage it.

When Cadel realised he had to stop and change bikes, he didn't go into crisis mode. 'I was concentrating on what I had to do. That's probably experience ... stay calm, do what you've got to do ...' he told the *Sydney Morning Herald* in an interview in Melbourne during his visit to Australia for his victory parade:

It's happened to me where I have had some bad luck, moments where I could have won the Tour of Spain, the Tour de France ... but when I go back to the team thing, everyone around is calm and everyone is doing their best—don't get nervous, don't panic, because things are going to go wrong. We do what we can. That's part of the process.

In the end that mechanical problem ended up becoming a bit of a blessing in disguise because of the way the race unfolded after that, but at that moment I was thinking, 'Oh-oh ... This isn't working. Something has gone wrong, find a way to fix the problem, let's get on with it'. Afterwards, when we looked back on it, it was, 'how did we not panic there?'

If I was to stay in front on that particular day, on the Col de Télégraphe with Contador, Schleck and Voeckler—they were riding at good speed, good pace ... they were eliminating all the other people that would have helped them later on.

Voeckler, [by] trying to stay on, actually exhausted himself early in the race ... For me that was great, because it was one less guy in front of me on GC—I moved up one place. But that also put the Schleck brothers in a position where they had to ride for the yellow.

After Cadel changed bikes the group came back to him. Basso's Liquigas team had panicked by then, and was riding quite hard behind. The other BMC riders were all struggling a bit, but they were in front, ready to go, when they saw Cadel in the distance as they rode up. Burghardt had been in the front and had dropped back by then, and Cadel started riding with him.

The others came back. Liquigas and BMC were there to ride—there were eight or 10 committed. Basso had no choice but to ride, because Cunego was in front, putting on the pressure.

That would have got Cadel up the last 18 kilometres of the 2556 metre–altitude climb safely, but he misjudged the final kilometres to the top.

In the last 6 or 8 kilometres the route gets very steep and very high, but Cadel had assumed they'd be going over the top to where the finish had been the day before. That was the ideal place to make up time, and BMC started to ride flat-out to the steep section.

Liquigas had a similar plan. They were all working together, but the BMC riders were climbing a bit better, and started to eliminate the Liquigas riders. There was really no alternative: BMC couldn't afford to ride more slowly. When they reached the bottom of the steep section, Cadel went alone, thinking that they were going over the top.

Cadel's misjudgement of the climb's summit from the northern side of the Galibier (at 2556 metres altitude as opposed to the 2645 metres altitude of the stage 19 finish) meant that he and his teammates had been expending energy at the wrong time. His timing also meant he came across a flatter section when he'd expected a steeper part of the climb to take back more time on his rivals.

Cadel needed to go flat-out on the descent. Sánchez had a bit of a gap on him, and started. The road is small; on one side there's a drop of a few hundred metres, and on the other side is a wall. Many of the corners are hidden until the barriers or signs saying 'sharp corner' become visible, so having a point of reference in front—particularly an excellent descender like Sánchez—is always a bonus.

The descent was fast but it was still into the headwind that went over the Col du Lautaret the previous day. While the wind wasn't as strong as the day before, when riders are chasing into the wind they need to pedal a lot and accelerate. Cadel was trying to close down Sánchez, accelerating at full speed out of every corner and attacking while trying to quickly grab something to eat or drink and get back up to speed again.

The sight of Cadel charging down the Col du Galibier at top speed may have prompted some to believe he was gliding down and saving energy. But the effort and energy used in descending can be underestimated.

Cadel was a little behind when Sánchez got back to the group, but Garmin had ridden very strongly down the valley, and they came back—which was in Cadel's favour. He'd expended quite a bit of energy to get back to the group, and Garmin made the difference until the road got steeper before Bourg d'Oisans.

On the run to Bourg d'Oisans and the foot of l'Alpe d'Huez, Cadel's group caught Contador and Andy Schleck. Cadel didn't waste any time in securing a strong position near the front, which minimised his chances of being exposed by an attack and forced to chase as he'd had to the day before.

With his time loss the day before, Contador had basically conceded that his hopes of an overall win were dashed; so when he attacked, observers felt it was an attempt either to try and gain time and move up a place or two, or to win a stage. Either way, Contador was out of the GC for the first time, and was not a particular worry for Cadel.

Cadel still had the Schleck brothers to contend with, though, and was marking them. And then came the big moment in the final when Andy went and spoke to Cadel.

Cadel had every reason to be wary. It was on this very climb in the 2008 Tour that he'd had to contend with not only the brothers, but also their Spanish former teammate Carlos Sastre; together they launched a three-pronged attack against him when they hit this last climb in the same group.

None of them was in the yellow jersey this time, as Fränk Schleck was in 2008, and Andy Schleck became the virtual leader on the road when Voeckler dropped back. But Cadel could not allow himself to be forced into chasing an attack by Fränk Schleck or a countermove by Andy.

And it didn't take long for the fun and games to begin. As the group wound its way up the 28 switchbacks that comprise the 14-kilometre climb, in the wake of Rolland and Contador, Cadel was suddenly asked by Andy Schleck if he would work with them. It was a moment that millions around the world watching on television tried to lip-read.

Cadel was taken aback by Schleck's request, to say the least. Voeckler was already dropped and Andy was going to ride into the yellow jersey, so as his competitor Cadel was certainly not going to help him.

It was not in Cadel's interests to let Andy or Fränk Schleck out of his sight. He wanted to take back some time, but he had already spent a fair bit of energy getting to the last climb. It was a short stage. He was there in front, but it was a hard start and a hard middle.

Andy Schleck's request on l'Alpe d'Huez could have been viewed as a signal that he was insecure about how strongly positioned he really was to achieve an overall victory—but there was always the possibility that he was playing a game and would suddenly attack.

It later became one of the most hotly discussed issues of the Tour because so many people saw the exchange live on television: what Andy Schleck said to Cadel. When asked during his visit home to Australia for his victory parade, Cadel told the media:

> I didn't say much. Andy was asking to ride together … and [about] co-operating with them. After the day before, I wasn't going to be co-operative. I had no obligation to.
>
> I can recall pretty much word for word, and it's probably best that I don't repeat the words exactly … a little bit of colourful language. But I have a lot of respect for, particularly, Andy. He is someone I have always had a good

relationship [with] even though we are competitors. He was in a difficult situation and needed help from me ... I was in a situation where I wasn't obligated to do it, so I wasn't going to waste or compromise my race.

After already saving his Tour with a magnificent chase of Schleck on Stage 18 from Pinerolo to Galibier Serre-Chevalier, Cadel was well within his rights to ignore Schleck, who was in the box seat to take the yellow jersey from the fading Voeckler, not Evans. But mind games are part of the Tour, and Cadel had expected them on Stage 19:

> He had his teammate to ride him into the yellow jersey and put him in a position to win the Tour. They were in a position ... [he] had a teammate, and I was on my own, and I already had my problems for the day. I had been put in difficulty. So for me it was completely up to them [to chase Contador].

Andy Schleck gave his version of events when he spoke to a gathering of journalists on an ocean ferry during a rough-and-tumble stage transfer in the 2012 Tour of Oman. He was reported as saying:

> I didn't ask Cadel if he would work for me. I said there are three guys up the road, [and that] Alberto Contador can take [places on] the GC. I was riding so I asked if [Cadel] would ride also because it was not only my place [in danger] but his place. But he wouldn't agree which I certainly understand ... but it doesn't hurt to ask, no?

Either way, it seemed more likely LeOpard would play Andy's card in its bid for the Tour, based on his time-trialling ability; still, even on the Col d'Izoard the day before, observers had thought Fränk would attack. But no-one could be certain, and the Schlecks played with that well.

• • •

How riders manage to negotiate their way through the crowds on l'Alpe d'Huez never ceases to amaze, but in 2011 many felt the intensity and size of the Tour's most famous crowd had reached unprecedented levels. Not that there was any sense of danger or fear, but the anticipation that resonated from those who had spent days camped on one of sport's most outstanding grandstands appeared stronger than in years.

When the time comes for riders to fight out such crucial phases in the Tour, the intensity of competition between them helps to black out fear of a spectator-caused disaster like the one in 1999. Italian Giuseppe Guerini (Telekom) fell on l'Alpe d'Huez with about 1 kilometre to go in a race-winning solo attack when he collided with a fan who had stood out to take his photo face-on, froze when he realised his error, and subsequently brought both of them down.

Riders learn when to tap into the enthusiasm of the crowd and to switch off from it. Sometimes the crowd is there to lift them; other times they can't afford to get carried away because they need to concentrate on the race.

Riders don't talk to each other very much, but there's a lot of noise on the mountain. When the pressure is intense, the noise can intrude, but focusing on it can create a psychologically negative situation.

There are people who try and do anything they can to put a rider off. Sometimes it's with sniping remarks, sometimes there are protests, and sometimes there's someone holding up a really offensive sign. A potent reminder of this is the picture of Contador hitting a spectator who had badgered him as the Tour climbed l'Alpe d'Huez on stage 20; he was dressed in a surgeon's cape and mask and attempted to take Contador's heart rate with a stethoscope as he ran alongside him.

The innuendo of it was clear: Contador's doping case, relating to his positive test for clenbuterol during the 2010 Tour he won, was still before the Court of Arbitration for Sport (CAS). In February 2012 Contador was banned for two years by the CAS; the ban was retroactive, and he was told he could return to racing in 5 August the same year. However, the CAS finding also declared that he should be stripped of his 2010 Tour title, and any wins from 2011.

Cadel has not made any judgement on the CAS hearing, its finding or the defence put forward by the Contador camp; or on the appeals lodged by the Union Cycliste Internationale and the World Anti-Doping Agency against the Spanish federation's February 2011 decision to clear him and allow him to race. However, Cadel has made no secret of the fact that he has grown to respect the Spaniard.

Contador's mental strength is obvious. It is impressive that he finished the Tour when he could have withdrawn from the race, or ridden with less panache in light of the attention directed at him on the lead-up into the Tour. He continued in spite of being jeered at by crowds; and he didn't take the myriad get-outs presented by his crashes during the race and the knee injury he carried through the Tour.

Cadel was also happy Contador raced, despite the debate over whether he should take part because of the postponed CAS hearing into his doping case. With Contador having raced, no one could throw the 'what if' question at him— which might have happened had the Spaniard decided not to try to defend his Tour title. Asked if that was the case, Cadel said:

> In some ways, yeah … This year in some ways I was a little bit underestimated going into the Tour by some of my competitors, but that has its advantages. When you are painted up as the favourite, everyone is looking at you.

• • •

Over the last kilometres on l'Alpe d'Huez, Cadel continued to monitor the Schlecks, who set about limiting the time Contador got on them. He could have attacked them, but the energy he had expended earlier would have magnified the risks and limitations of such an action.

He was struggling a little bit more than on the stage to Galibier Serre-Chevalier, but it was a hard day for everyone. Cadel didn't have the exclusivity at that point in the race to get a gap—and there were two of them. The challenge would have been to bring them back and counterattack afterwards. A 2- or 3-kilometre effort would not have made a substantial difference—possibly a 10-second gap. The energy he had left could be better saved for the next day's time trial in Grenoble.

Rolland won at the summit finish on l'Alpe d'Huez by 14 seconds from Sánchez and 23 seconds from Contador, who finished 34 seconds clear of fifth-placed Cadel and the Schleck brothers. For the Schlecks the result was still one to savour.

Andy Schleck, ninth on the stage, took the yellow jersey from Voeckler, while Fränk was second overall at 53 seconds. The mood among their supporters at the ski station town that night was one of jubilation. At one particular bar, their fans partied the night away, as if they had already won the Tour. Andy Schleck knew it was a daunting prospect to defend his 57-second lead on Cadel, now third overall; but he also saw it as confirmation of his career goal to win the Tour.

After the stage, Cadel and his teammates rode slowly to their hotel—the Club Med a few kilometres away on the eastern outskirts of l'Alpe d'Huez—to begin their customary recovery. Cadel knows the hotel well, as he has stayed there during previous Tours. Approaching the hotel, Cadel rode right through the open doorway and into the reception area where Andy Rihs, his brother, Jim Ochowicz and the BMC team soigneuse Trudi Rebsamen were waiting. He rode into the doorway so he'd have 2 metres less to walk.

The atmosphere at the hotel that night was hardly relaxed. The Club Med is one of the largest hotels on the mountain and has notoriously small rooms. It was also full of riders and staff from other teams, and members of the Tour entourage that ranged from the podium girls to sponsors' representatives, advertising caravan staff and some media. Cadel and his teammates had their pasta cooked as usual by chef Peter Cambre.

Cadel failed to get the good night's sleep that he had hoped for on the eve of the biggest ride of his career. Not only was the room frustratingly cramped, but the calm of night was drowned out by music from a nightclub.

One perplexing aspect of the Tour is that everyone but the winner gets criticised—but no-one attracts more criticism than the rider who comes second. Cadel has experienced that twice—in 2007, when he was second to Contador by 23 seconds, and in 2008, when Sastre beat him by 58 seconds. It was a fate that awaited him or Andy Schleck after the next day's time trial, Schleck also having twice placed second overall in the Tour. It was not lost on observers that while Cadel or Schleck would clinch a breakthrough Tour win, a third runner-up finish awaited the other.

It was an accomplishment for Cadel, who has encountered the Schleck two-up throughout his career, that he was able to overcome the danger they presented on l'Alpe d'Huez. The last time he'd ridden there was against Carlos Sastre; he did what he could on the day but was beaten by Sastre and a very good team. It was a difficult situation and he handled it well, but his second-place overall attracted the usual criticism.

As much as Cadel remembers that day in 2008 as clear as if it were yesterday, being able to return to l'Alpe d'Huez with a ride that went a long way towards securing him his—and Australia's—first ever victory in the Tour was as fitting a comeback to the fabled mountain as anyone could have wished for.

Sure, he didn't win the stage. He wasn't in the yellow jersey. But with one time trial to go, and in third place overall at 57 seconds to Andy Schleck, the likelihood was that his time in the sun was very close. If he was to get the yellow jersey, it would be for the final ride into Paris.

And when it came to an individual race against the clock, like the time trial in Grenoble the next day, he was finally the master of his own destiny.

15

THE DAY OF TRUTH

Cadel Evans, John Lelangue and Steve Morabito left the BMC hotel at l'Alpe d'Huez as early as possible—7.30 am—for Grenoble, where the Tour's final time trial was to be held, in an effort to avoid the traffic congestion. It was a shift in habit for Cadel, whose time-trial start was due at 4.12 pm. He would normally have enjoyed a sleep-in before such a major stage, but after a night of much commotion on l'Alpe d'Huez, he was hardly rested.

Even though they'd left early—two hours earlier than they'd thought was necessary—they had to wait at a tunnel for hours, and so arrived in Grenoble with only just enough time. In the last year or two in the Tour, there have often been big traffic jams in transfers.

It was a masterstroke that Cadel left l'Alpe d'Huez as early as he did—teammates who travelled later were held up so severely that some feared they may miss their start. Although, were it not for Tour rules requiring everyone to stay in their official hotel, it would have been wiser to leave the night before and stay in Grenoble. But doing so would have been a serious breach of the regulations, and one that organisers would not have treated lightly. In 1994 the Swiss rider Urs Zimmermann (Motorola) was lucky to avoid being kicked off the Tour after he made an official transfer on the eve of the rest day by car—because of his fear of flying—rather than on the plane that had been chartered by the race. He stayed overnight at a hotel on the road, and were it not for a local paper publishing a photo of him eating dinner there, no-one would have been the wiser for it. But when the race organisers saw the news clipping, they came down on Zimmermann and the team.

At first Zimmermann faced being sent home. There was a long meeting at the race office in Pau between Motorola manager Jim Ochowicz (now president of Cadel's BMC team) and then–Tour director Jean-Marie Leblanc. It took place in a windowed office that virtually turned their meeting into a silent movie for an observing media. Race organisers backed down and instead suspended Ochowicz from the Tour for a day.

Cadel sat for hours in the car in the tunnel, waiting to go through. When he arrived everyone was a bit nervous. It was the big time trial—Cadel's big race—and it could perhaps even win him the Tour.

Morabito and Cadel went for a final ride over the Grenoble course, with Lelangue following in a BMC team car. The ride was aimed at reacquainting Cadel with the route difficulties and technical aspects in the prevailing weather conditions, rather than to reveal anything new. It was also to help him switch mentally into his time-trial mode. Cadel had already raced over the course in the Critérium du Dauphiné in June, and he had studied it closely on maps and in discussions throughout the year with Lelangue, who recalls how thorough their last reconnaissance of the route was:

> Making the first roundabout before the first climb, we were assessing taking the right side, and then Cadel said, 'Don't you think it's better on the left side?' I said, 'Oh, I'll do a U-turn' ... he'll go through each detail of all the different options.

Cadel rode over the course on a dry run before the 4 kilometre–long Tour advertising caravan set off for its penultimate parade before a typically massive crowd that lined the route. It was imperative to get there before the publicity caravan, because when it's on the course it's quite dangerous.

The course itself tested everything. It had long, flat straights; reasonably hard climbs; fast, technical downhills; some pave (cobblestones); left and right turns; and long, false flats. The bike set-up needed to cover everything.

Crucial to advising Cadel was former rider Italian Stefano Cattai, who had worked with Cadel in the wind tunnel and velodrome tests on his position and the new time-trial bike. It was suggested that Cadel should use specialist time-trial tyres due to the warm, dry weather. Cadel, however, decided to use standard road tyres. That way he could go into all the corners with full confidence and on tyres he'd been riding on for the whole race, even if they were a bit slower. That was the last piece of equipment fine-tuning they did.

After his final preparations, Cadel sat in the bus listening to music, and had a bit of rest. He had some lunch that Peter Cambre had prepared after a light breakfast at the hotel, and then he waited.

He spoke to teammates returning from their time trials, went for a final test ride to ensure his bike was as he wanted it, and then returned to the team bus. Later he came out, got on his bike and started to ride on the rollers, because by that time he was starting to concentrate on warming up. The crowd outside was building.

• • •

In the crowd that built up while Cadel warmed up were his Australian agent Jason Bakker, Sydney businessman David Paradice, and a number of associates connected with Australia's first ever World Tour team. Orica-GreenEDGE was still then a 'project', and five months from learning whether its application for a first-division ProTeam licence for the 2012 season had been accepted by the UCI.

Cadel, while contracted to BMC and having declared that he would probably ride out his career with the US-registered team, had been an open supporter of the Australian Orica-GreenEDGE project. In May, the day after returning to his home in Stabio, Switzerland, from a high-altitude training camp, he had attended a Orica-GreenEDGE media conference at its base—the Australian Institute of Sport's European Training Centre at Gavirate in Varese, which had opened in March that year.

To the seasoned observer, the crowd was a window into the world of professional cycling, particularly the winking-and-nodding between various parties involved in various deals that tend to be conducted and negotiated in cycling throughout a Tour. With this Tour nearing its end, so too were many deals—including rider recruitment, though UCI rules don't allow recruiting before August. Conversations between riders, directors, sponsors and people associated with Orica-GreenEDGE led to much speculation.

• • •

The attention of onlookers while warming up can be distracting, if a rider lets it get to him. Some riders spend up to 90 minutes warming up on the rollers in a carefully planned process requiring them to reach certain heart rates at certain points in time, and while riding certain gears. It varies widely, of course, depending on what each rider's body needs, and on their levels of fatigue—it's important to do enough, but not too much. With experience, riders get to know what works for them in different weather conditions—they'll have a warm-up for a one-day race, one for the prologue and mid-way in the Tour, and a different one for the end of a three-week race. Cadel's pre-time-trial ritual was 20 to 30 minutes long and was based on feel.

Riders try hard not to read too much into their warm-up—sometimes they'll feel great at warm-up, only to find that they're far from their best in the race, and vice versa.

After warming up, Cadel went into the bus and got changed, put his helmet and glasses on and then set off for the start line. Most riders try and leave the bus as close to their start time as possible, optimally arriving at the start line a minute before—but with bike checks and crowds it takes longer. The bigger the race, the more compromised the warm-up can be.

Cadel left the BMC bus for the starting ramp a few hundred metres away. Everyone in the BMC team was calm, including Cadel. He had a really good bike, he was riding well, he was in a great position, and all the equipment that BMC had been developing and refining was working well. All the work had been done, and everything was prepared.

Cadel felt better than the last time he was about to start a time trial knowing he was within grasp of overall victory in the Tour—in 2008, when he was second overall at 1 minute 34 seconds to Spaniard Carlos Sastre (CSC), who had taken the yellow jersey on l'Alpe d'Huez the day before. Almost everyone had expected Cadel to make up his gap on Sastre in the 53-kilometre stage 20 time trial, and fend off all the other challengers.

In every third-week Tour time trial over a similar distance since 2005, he had beaten Sastre by between 1 minute 4 seconds and 2 minutes 33 seconds. In the 29.5-kilometre stage 4 time trial at Cholet in 2008 he beat Sastre by 1 minute 16 seconds, which prompted an estimation that he would beat Sastre in the 53-kilometre stage 20 time trial by 2 minutes 30 seconds. A poll of 15 sports directors that year tipped Cadel to beat Sastre by 3 minutes—as did Belgian great Eddy Merckx, and even Sastre's Australian teammate Stuart O'Grady. But it was not to be. It was clear early into his time trial that Cadel was out of sorts, as he seemed to struggle with the bike. Eventually he could only better Sastre by 29 seconds.

Before the 2011 time trial Cadel was calm; observers felt he had the form to win. He even played down the billing of the time trial as the 'race of truth', simplifying the discipline in an interview with the *Sydney Morning Herald*, saying, 'It's as if you have to do it and stay calm and go as hard as possible'. But then his attention to detail emerged:

> You are only riding a bike from point A to point B, but in terms of technique there is much in terms of pedalling, breathing—and there are the corners. Just to concentrate and ride out beyond your limit is very taxing actually. It's more technical but you are also trying to get it out physically. Extracting the two—both at once—is emotionally and mentally quite draining.

In light of Andy Schleck's deficiencies in the time trial, it was only logical to believe that if Cadel won the stage he would get the yellow jersey. So the immediate target for Cadel was not Schleck, but German time-trial specialist Tony Martin (HTC-Highroad), who had won the Dauphiné time trial in June. Hence John Lelangue agreed to provide Cadel with time checks against Martin—who began 66 minutes before him—rather than against Schleck.

Cadel was the third-last rider to start, and was followed by second-placed Fränk Schleck 3 minutes later and Andy Schleck 6 minutes later.

Other teammates who had raced over the course in the warm, humid conditions of the day advised Cadel to start the stage conservatively because the climb was difficult, but it became apparent that he intended to start hard on the flat and gain time early.

After the first climb to the 9-kilometre mark at Brie-et-Angonnes, where a BMC staffer and former rider Scott Nydam was stationed to record his personal split, Cadel took the descent at high speed into Vizille at 15 kilometres and through a tunnel, after which there was the first official time check.

Behind Cadel in the BMC team car was Lelangue, who could see he was pushing it on the rough road and feared he would crash when his bike began to shake.

On television it might have looked quite smooth, but there were potholes and it was rough coming into the village. There was a sharp left turn into the tunnel where it was extremely rough on one side, so when Cadel came out he went over to the other side to the good line. At the time check he was 20 seconds down on Martin, but he could see someone in front of him—Thomas Voeckler.

Voeckler, at fourth overall, started the stage 3 minutes before Cadel. Cadel also knew that behind him were the Schleck brothers—Fränk, who started 3 minutes behind him, and Andy, who began 6 minutes behind him. Cadel was going flat out on the flats to not lose time and then attacking to make time on the climb.

Cadel was 8 to 10 minutes into his time trial before receiving time checks on Andy Schleck, who was the last to start. After about 5 kilometres he was already cutting back the time on Schleck. Then, at the first official mark, at 15 kilometres, Cadel's split of 20 minutes 33 seconds was second-fastest, and 33 seconds ahead of Schleck's time of 21 minutes 9 seconds. But by the second official time check, on top of the climb to Saint-Martin-d'Uriage after 27.5 kilometres, he was 6 seconds behind Martin. Cadel was also up on Schleck by 1 minute 42 seconds. But after that, and on the descent towards Grenoble, Cadel did not receive any further time checks from Lelangue, who was urging him not to take any risks. Cadel backed off very slightly.

The descent was still high speed and tricky and included a left turn at a roundabout followed by a right, left, right, right, sharp-left switchback—and a sweeping corner before straightening out. Cadel took the next few corners a bit slow after momentarily losing concentration when he saw a man by the road; but then he got going again on the downhill. He nailed it, even though there were potholes at one point—he went to lift over them, then went flying up through the air.

From there Cadel powered into the last 3 kilometres of the stage, and then backed off slightly—and that might have been the difference between winning the stage and not. When he rode into the finish he was quite calm.

History shows that Cadel had good reason to fear a crash. In 2005 Danish rider Michael Rasmussen was third overall and vying for a podium finish in the final stage 20 time-trial when nerves got the better of him—he crashed after

4 kilometres, then had two bike changes followed by two wheel changes, and then crashed into a ditch to drop to seventh place overall. Then, in the 100th Giro d'Italia in 2009, Russian Denis Menchov was wearing the race leader's pink jersey when he crashed in wet and slippery conditions in the last time trial, close to the finish in Rome.

However, this time Cadel enjoyed a safe passage to the line. He crossed it with a finishing time of 55 minutes 40 seconds, and suddenly found himself in the eye of a storm of impending celebration as they waited for Andy Schleck to finish.

Cadel had been trying to work out what his time was, but everyone around him was a little too excited. Then Schleck arrived.

After all those years of setbacks and coming second and second again, and the criticism that came with that—all of a sudden everything turned around. Cadel seemed calm, but everyone around him was beside themselves.

Cadel still didn't know where to go, or what he had to do or who he was talking to. People who'd followed him for years were really happy. Journalists came up and peppered him with questions.

One person who had not yet joined in the celebration was Lelangue. He was sitting alone in the BMC car and watching Schleck's final kilometres on a television screen. He says:

In respect for the yellow jersey I wanted to wait. I didn't want to explode before it was won. But when it was won … I cried a bit. Then I went to the team bus, straight to the guys … you know, it was the fulfilment of a project that had begun several years back.

It wasn't just the two years with Cadel, but ever since 2007 when we built the ProContinental team planning to one day go to the Tour, then to win the Tour. It was an amateur team in 2007. We did the Tour de Friuli, which is an amateur race. We had one car, one minibus, one mechanic and one soigneur. We were eating in little hotels with amateur riders. That was the beginning. That was the BMC/Californian team being in Europe. Then the year after, in 2008, we were ProContinental with only Swiss and Americans ... And then we grew up, step by step.

When Cadel returned to the BMC team bus, the mood was one of elation. His teammates had all sat and watched Cadel ride on television. American Brent Bookwalter, a rider who had been with BMC since 2008, and who also rode for Cadel in his 2010 Giro and Tour, recalls:

The Tour tests me in ways that I never thought I would—or could—be tested. It's brought me to my knees and to my total wits' end, time and again. Then when we were watching Cadel ride that time trial of his life, it was hard to believe it was happening—all those feelings, the pain, frustration, even bitterness at times, all melted away. I think I spent as much energy watching his ride as I did out there earlier in the day, doing my own, because we were just sweating you know, and grabbing each other, willing him forward as fast as we could.

When Cadel returned to the bus after the yellow jersey presentation and the press conference that the soon-to-be Tour winner traditionally gives on the eve of the last stage, he saw his parents-in-law, Luisa and Aldo, happily celebrating with his teammates and team staff, who were all drinking beers. Cadel's wife, Chiara, was in Paris and had watched the stage on television from her hotel room.

Back in the Grenoble velodrome, where Cadel had spoken to the media, journalists were busily writing their reports of his imminent overall victory.

As a smiling Cadel entered the velodrome in his yellow jersey and carrying the Credit Lyonnaise lion that all yellow-jersey wearers are awarded, he received a warm applause that—because of the series of doping controversies that had plagued past editions and their winners—had not been heard for several years.

Cadel was still cautious about celebrating an imminent Tour victory—he is not one to count his chickens before they are hatched. But he understood the reasoning behind the press conference being dubbed the 'winner's' press conference because of all the protocol and activity that comes on the last day in Paris. It was also a huge reminder of the difference that comes with making that step up from second to first overall.

Seasoned riders usually have an idea of what some questions will be after the first couple of words, and will have the answer ready to go. Cadel is known for being upfront and honest; sometimes it rubs people the wrong way. He was asked whether he was going to win the Tour, to which he answered 'I don't know'. After all, the Tour is not a staged race. It's a real race, and no-one knows what's going to happen.

However, Cadel certainly didn't hide his emotion when asked about how much of a role his former trainer Aldo Sassi had played in his success. As he spoke, his eyes welled up and he hesitated between some sentences. The silence among the media was golden. Even his detractors could not help but respect the moment. As much as he may have been prepared for questions, and as obvious as it might have been that one of them would be about Sassi, he was caught by a flood of emotion when it was actually asked of him:

> It was Aldo Sassi who believed in me. He often believed in me more than I did, and for a friend to be here today would be …
>
> When we won [the world titles] at Mendrisio, it was 6 kilometres from his house—the finish line. It was a beautiful day there … he said to me at one point last year, 'I'm sure you can win a grand tour. I hope for you it's the Tour de France because that's the most prestigious tour. But if you do, you'll become the most complete rider of your generation' … and, um … for him today to see me now would be quite something.

Elite riders need to be able to contain and control their emotions, but sometimes it's not possible. And sometimes it's better when they don't. That value was brought home to Cadel the year before, on the day after the Tour finished with him still in the peloton, having broken his elbow on the stage he claimed the yellow jersey for a day. One of the official Tour podium girls approached Cadel and Chiara at the airport in Paris and thanked him for being human and showing his emotions—because sport needs that.

One thing that still left some journalists hankering for greater elaboration after Cadel left the press conference in the Grenoble velodrome was his position on doping. Cadel has long been regarded—from within and outside the peloton—as a clean rider; but also he has long remained tight-lipped about his views on the issue and those who are caught for it, other than to applaud efforts to crack down on the problem. It was felt by a number of journalists that as the soon-to-be Tour champion, he was in a position to take a greater stand on the issue.

Cadel's thinking is that if he leads a proper and correct career as an athlete who is consistently tested and has been consistently performing at an extremely high level, then that should stand as just as much of a message against doping as any words do. Similarly, in such a case, he feels that he doesn't have anything to answer to or prove. His result should say enough.

Cadel had done all that at Grenoble. He was 24 hours away from being officially declared as the Tour champion, and had yet to absorb the enormity of a feat that had been likened to Australia's 1983 America's Cup win—one of Australian sport's last frontiers. Asked what he felt about claiming the Tour's leader's jersey in a time trial to secure a virtually insurmountable lead—and for his thoughts on its comparison to the America's Cup victory, Cadel said:

I would have to have been pretty young back then. I don't think we even had a TV. Between now and the Champs Elysées I have time to digest everything. Now I'm keen to go to the [team] bus and have a little 'chin chin' with the guys.

After beating Schleck's overall lead of 57 seconds, he still had one more day to race before he could really look at himself in the mirror and say he was the Tour champion. But his second place in the time trial, at 7 seconds to Martin, had him in the yellow leader's jersey as planned. He would start the 95-kilometre 21st stage, from Créteil to the Champs Elysées in Paris, with an overall lead of 1 minute 34 seconds on Andy Schleck, and 2 minutes 30 seconds on Fränk Schleck.

Even before he left for Paris everyone was applauding Cadel, who was so close to making history. Only four times in the past 50 years had anyone come from behind to take the Tour lead in the final time trial as he did. And, at the age of 34, Cadel was poised to become the second-oldest ever Tour winner.

16

THE FINAL RIDE

Cadel Evans knew that he had to remain focused for the final stage into Paris after taking the yellow jersey from Andy Schleck in Grenoble. However, he had learned in 2007, when Alberto Contador led the race in the last day with a slender 23-second lead, that overcoming such a deficit is unthinkable in a normal road stage, because it is traditionally one for the sprinters and is controlled by their teams. The race is so fast that for an overall contender to attack a peloton that is racing at almost 60 kilometres per hour, and then stay away to the finish with a lead equivalent to or better than their starting deficit, is next to impossible. The only realistic way a rider can take the yellow jersey from the race leader on the last day is if the stage is a time trial. And the Tour has not had a final-day time trial since 1989, when the American Greg LeMond—in 1986 the first non-European to win the Tour—came from 50 seconds down to beat the French race leader Laurent Fignon, the 1983 champion, and win by a record low of 8 seconds.

In 2011, Cadel was already regarded as the Tour-winner-in-waiting when he joined teammates in their Grenoble hotel after the time trial.

Arriving at the hotel in the BMC car with John Lelangue and Jim Ochowicz after the 'race winner's' press conference, Cadel was met by fans and friends. One of the first supporters he saw was a Belgian named Lucien, a man who regularly appears at the summit of the last climb of any day, standing next to his van adorned with a Belgian flag with the words *Qui est le Lion?* (Who is the Lion?). Lucien offers bottled water to riders in need on mountain tops. And while Cadel does not usually accept them, he appreciates the man's loyalty and dedication to helping the riders.

For the last three weeks, Cadel's personal osteopath David Bombeke had been carrying one of Cadel's 2009 world champion's jerseys—that Cadel had signed and inscribed with 'Qui est le Lion?'—in readiness to give it to Lucien as thanks for his support of the riders. He had been carrying this jersey for about three weeks, and finally they saw him.

One unexpected request for Cadel came at about 8 pm, before dinner when he was on the massage table nearing the end of his nightly rub-down by Bombeke. When his mobile rang, Cadel noticed the international country code on the screen and saw it was a Luxembourg number. He didn't take the call, but soon he received a text message that had come from Andy Schleck. Cadel was curious to know what it was about and called Schleck back. Cadel was pleasantly surprised that Schleck simply wanted to congratulate him on his Tour win, and after a short chat the pair pledged to one day share a beer together—which they did at the US Pro Challenge in Colorado.

Also in the celebratory mayhem of the hotel that night was a Belgian television crew, there to do an arranged live interview with Cadel before he finally ate dinner with his teammates in a private room; the team had to close the door to ensure they had some privacy to appreciate the day's outcome and toast it with a glass of champagne. Fans, understandably, were keen to congratulate Cadel, but it was the first time he'd had a chance to sit with his teammates and they were keen to avoid interruption.

Another surprise that night came after dinner when Cadel was in the bath. He had just lain down and was enjoying the silence and solitude when his mobile rang—it was Australian Prime Minister Julia Gillard.

Cadel had already spoken to the Opposition leader, Tony Abbott, who is an avid cyclist and who had contacted Cadel before the stage to wish him well. But it had been arranged that Prime Minister Gillard would telephone Cadel after the job was done and dinner had been eaten, when he was relaxed. In all the excitement, Cadel had forgotten all about it.

As Cadel stood in a hastily thrown-on hotel bathrobe with his still-damp yellow jersey hanging on the bathroom chair, Gillard told him he'd been an inspiration to countless Australians, and that she hoped he would be able to come home to celebrate. Hearing from the Australian prime minister that the country was behind him could only have given him a boost.

•   •   •

It was an early start the next day. The entire peloton was flown on a Qatar Airways A330 from Grenoble to Paris for the start of the 21st and final stage to the Champs Elysées in Paris.

One of Cadel's first official duties before he boarded the plane from the tarmac at Grenoble was to sign a yellow jersey for the airline's chief executive officer, Akbar Al Baker. Once on board, Cadel took the window seat on the left front row with his teammate Ivan Santaromita and a bundle of memorabilia that had been passed to him by sponsors and well-wishers—one being a stuffed white toy dog that looked exactly like Snowy, the beloved mutt of the fabled cartoon character Tintin, who Cadel has often said is his only hero. On the other side of the plane was five-time Tour winner Bernard Hinault, then still the last Frenchman to win the Tour, and Belgian legend Eddy Merckx. It was not a quiet flight north. Cadel was kept busy doing interviews with select media outlets who travelled on the flight.

The flight was a short one, and Cadel arrived hungry. Fortunately, BMC team chef Peter Cambre had thought ahead and had prepared one of his on-the-road meals for Cadel to eat once he'd arrived in Paris. It's easy to miss breakfast when you're doing interviews on the plane, and the last thing Cadel needed was to go hunger-flat in the ride to Paris.

The stage start on the last day of the Tour de France is always a circus. For the peloton, it is like the last day at school—every rider can mentally see the finish. Despite the highs and lows they have experienced in getting to the last-stage start line, they all feel a sense of pride knowing that they will finish the Tour—and before a crowd that numbers in thousands, on one of the world's most well-known and picturesque boulevards: the Champs Elysées.

Of course, for the sprinters in the peloton and their teams, there is also the excitement of taking one more crack at a stage win. For Cadel on this day in 2011, there must have been a sense of anxiety. While Schleck had conceded defeat to him the night before, he still needed to finish the stage safely and in the peloton.

Hence, when his team handed him a yellow BMC bike to ride for the occasion, he baulked. The fear of something going horribly wrong on a bike he had not ridden before—and with it painted yellow—was simply too great. He had already experienced the hazard of a premature celebration: in the 2008 Tour, after he took the yellow jersey on stage 10 while riding for Davitamon-Lotto, there had been a lavish outdoor press conference and champagne garden-party in which he was paraded to the media to the music of Men At Work. He finished second, for the second year in a row, 58 seconds shy of first.

If Cadel had ridden the yellow bike it would probably have been fine, but riding it for the first time on the closing stage of the Tour de France was not just tempting fate—it was also simply too great a risk. He agreed to ride it through the neutralised zone to the official start, but then switched back to the bike he had ridden all Tour. He'd ridden that bike so far, to get where he was—that being one stage away from creating Australian sporting history—and felt it deserved to be the bike that was ridden into Paris.

And it wasn't long before his caution was vindicated. It happened in the neutralised zone while re-positioning himself for one of the array of official photos: of him celebrating his imminent victory by raising a plastic flute filled with champagne; and with other soon-to-be declared winners of the green (points competition), white (best young rider) and red-and-white polka dot (King of the Mountains) jerseys. As he moved to the BMC car to raise a glass of bubbly with John Lelangue, the television motorbike in front of him fell. Cadel was lucky to avoid it.

As it happened, when the stage hit the Champs Elysées about two hours later, one of the jersey winners riding a specially made—and untested—bike the colour of their jersey actually experienced Cadel's worst fear and had to stop for a mechanical problem.

Once order was restored, Cadel was back on his standard bike and the stage unfolded as it always does—at a helter-skelter pace that belies any perception that it is just a 'procession' ending with the 'inevitable' bunch sprint; the Australian was able to prepare for the greatest moment of his career.

As the early kilometres passed under their pedals, the peloton's anticipation grew. The riders were waiting for that first sighting of the Eiffel Tower as they hit the River Seine for the approach to the 6-kilometre finishing circuit on the Champs Elysées, which they race over eight times. As each kilometre passed, Cadel's place in cycling history firmed. Tradition is that the team of the yellow jersey leads the peloton en-masse as it arrives on the Champs Elysées—like the first regiment of a conquering army returning from battle. Cadel rallied his troops for their moment, giving them the honour of riding onto the Champs Elysées with the yellow jersey right near the front, and on their wheel.

The grande arrivée of the BMC team onto the Champs Elysées was among the highlights of Cadel's career. In the sport of cycling there's not much that compares with the last 3 kilometres before riding onto the Champs Elysées in the yellow jersey.

The BMC team did organise itself into position well for the entrance. And, fittingly, it was Hincapie who led the red-and-black BMC train onto the famous cobblestoned stretch. The experienced riders in the team knew that a massive roar from the crowd lining the barriers awaited—but when they got there, it almost blew them off their bikes.

Once on the finishing circuit and with the massive shift in ambience and emotions in order, Cadel resumed his focus on racing safely and just finishing. As long as he got within the last 3 kilometres—the mark where race organisers declare that the overall race has finished, to save contenders from being involved in the final bunch sprint for the stage win and risk crashing out—that his yellow jersey was safe. That last gallop home for the stage win was without a doubt one of the most frenetic and demanding bunch-sprint finishes of any Tour de France.

The 2011 finale in Paris was certainly no different, as it represented the last roll of the dice for teams to win something—either through brazen last-gasp attacks, or in the bunch sprint. Cadel placed fifty-sixth. Mark Cavendish won the stage and the points competition's green jersey for his soon-to-be-disbanded HTC-Highroad team by outsprinting Norway's Edvald Boasson Hagen (Sky) and German André Greipel (Omega Pharma-Lotto).

Cadel, wearing the yellow jersey, only had to finish in the bunch to secure his overall win—which he did with a winning time of 86 hours 12 minutes 22 seconds, 1 minute 34 seconds ahead of Andy Schleck (LeOpard) and 2 minutes 30 seconds clear of Fränk Schleck.

The scene at the finish, following the stage win by British sprinter Cavendish, was one of pandemonium as the BMC riders stopped near one another and then jumped on top of each other in celebration, as if they were a football team that had just scored the winning point.

The jubilation was a release of the pressure they'd been under to avoid any misfortune scuppering their victory. The worst-case scenario would have been a crash, at least before the 3-kilometre to go mark. Riders can and do run into trouble on the Champs Elysées. There have been crashes in the past, and punctures—and just that very day Cadel had seen one of the jersey holders have a mechanical problem. The cobblestones are very rough, people were tired—the BMC team just needed to stay safe.

Only when he had crossed the finish line did Cadel stop and smell the roses. The footy-style team hug was such an automatic thing—they had worked together through thick and thin since the year before, when Cadel had a fractured elbow and the team had ridden for him. Their belief in each other got them through that 2010 Tour, and was instrumental in leading them to victory in 2011.

Such a collective group celebration was a first for Hincapie:

> There was a lot of emotion. For me, we were just a small, relatively new, up-and-coming team, and less than two years later we were winning the biggest bike race in the world … it was a special moment. We all felt very proud.

• • •

Cadel was not the only Australian creating Tour history on the last day into Paris. Australian pop diva Tina Arena made a surprise appearance to sing the Australian national anthem, 'Advance Australia Fair', after Cadel was presented with the yellow jersey. Never before had a national anthem been sung—in past years, only the music of a national anthem had been played. Arena's performance was absolutely stunning and emotional for the fact it was unexpected, and also because of its significance.

To hear an Australian sing the national anthem on the Champs Elysées the year that an Australian first won the Tour—and with the Arc du Triomphe on a glorious, sunny Parisian summer afternoon as a backdrop—prompted a moving silence among the spectators. The silence held until Arena finished, and the trademark 'Aussie, Aussie, Aussie … oi, oi, oi' and cheers broke out among a crowd that included thousands of Australians waving national flags and blow-up Boxing Kangaroos.

Cadel didn't know anything about Arena's appearance beforehand: it was her idea. Arena is based in Paris, where she has become a popular and well-known figure in the music industry. She learned that Sunday morning about Cadel's imminent victory and the idea to sing the national anthem for the Tour presentation came to her. She felt so strongly about it that she made contact with Tour organisers through friends, and offered her services. The offer was quickly snapped up.

When Cadel heard someone was to sing the national anthem, he suspected it might be his wife Chiara, who is a gospel choir singer and had already surprised him by handing him an Australian flag that he wore draped around his neck. Then Arena, in a dark-blue T-shirt with an Australian flag on the front, appeared.

As Cadel stood on the podium during the anthem, the wave of emotion that swept through him was clearly visible. Winning the Tour de France was not just his dream, but quite possibly every bike rider's dream; and this was the first moment he'd been alone with his thoughts since he crossed the finish line.

Having stood on the podium position below him twice before, this was a moment he had earned and deserved. Before the decisive time trial in Grenoble, Cadel and Andy Schleck had known that one of them was going to end up a three-time second-place-getter, while the other would be celebrating a breakthrough win. It added to the moment for Cadel that Schleck had phoned him the night before the final stage after he had taken the yellow jersey from him. Sharing the podium with the Schleck brothers, Andy and third-placed Fränk, who were the first brothers ever to podium in the Tour, was an honour.

The official photo of Cadel with the Schlecks was not the only one that Cadel featured in. As he did at the start of the final stage when they were on bikes, Cadel also had a photo with the green jersey (points competition), Mark Cavendish; the red-and-white polka dot jersey (King of the Mountains), Spaniard Sammie Sánchez (Euskaltel-Euskadi); and the white jersey (best young rider), Frenchman Pierre Rolland (Europcar).

The image of the Australian flag Cadel wore around his neck wafting in the afternoon breeze—à la Superman— while Arena sang, was as majestic as any Tour winner's presentation ever held. After Arena sang, she passed the microphone to Cadel.

Cadel began his speech in French, thanking his fellow Australians, his team, all the public and everyone who had followed the Tour. After addressing the crowd in French, he seamlessly switched to English, and the Australians in the crowd leapt to their feet and cheered.

As Cadel stood there on the Champs Elysées, observers knew that he was experiencing the second fairy-tale scenario of his career in two years: to have stood atop the winner's dais at the world titles at Mendrisio, Switzerland, in 2009, and then on top of the podium at the Tour de France, was an incredible achievement.

It had been a dramatic turn of fortune for all involved in the BMC team; in 2009 it had been based in the United States and hoped to *race* in the 2010 Tour, let alone enjoy a day in yellow that year and then win it in 2011. BMC had been richly rewarded for their faith in Cadel.

When Cadel was 14 and first saw the Tour, he was quite taken with the Credit Lyonnaise lion that was given to the yellow jersey each day. Now he'd won his own. However, the Credit Lyonnaise lion Cadel has at home in Stabio is not the one he was presented with that Sunday 24 July in Paris—that one went to one of his most hard-working domestiques, German Marcus Burghardt, to give to his daughter. Burghardt's work for Cadel when the wind blew most dangerously was as vital to him winning the Tour as any element of his race. The lion at Cadel's house is, fittingly, from the Grenoble time trial.

When Cadel returned to the BMC bus, which was parked off the finishing circuit—in Rue Royale, which runs off the Rue de Rivoli shortly before the final turn to the 400-metre mark before the finish line—Cadel gave the lion to Burghardt. It was symbolic in more ways than one: on the same day the year before, Burghardt's wife had gone into labour with their first child.

Meanwhile, in the cordoned-off circle around the BMC bus soon after the stage, Cadel's teammates were in small groups with their partners and friends, drinking bottled beers and champagne in plastic flutes. Sitting alone in a red-and-black deck chair in the middle of the joyous scene was George Hincapie, who had just created his own chapter in

Tour history by taking the number of Tour-winning teams he had ridden for to nine. While elated for Cadel, Hincapie was also clearly proud of his achievement:

> It's such a hard event, and when you have somebody who can win, you always have to do the little things that people don't see. You always have to be aware. You have to be focused. You have to figure out what's going to happen up the road. It takes a lot of energy. To make it through nine is a very special feat.

Hincapie's sheer strength and size at the front of the peloton when riding tempo, or when riding to Cadel's side to protect him from the wind, was a massive help in achieving the end result. He was also vital in mustering the troops, organising who did what for Cadel, and for reading the race and co-ordinating tactics on the road. With his experience as a rider, he had become one of BMC's most valuable assets.

Hincapie was taken by Cadel's calmness under pressure. Asked to compare Cadel with Lance Armstrong and Alberto Contador, Hincapie says:

> They are the best athletes in the world. They are freaks of nature. They are mentally so strong, they don't let anything that comes along bother them. They are focused on one task. Their physical abilities—it's amazing how hard they can make the rest of us suffer, how meticulous they are in preparation, how good they are on the bikes. In that sense, they're all quite similar.

They also have very different personalities. I really didn't know Contador that well—we were only one year on the team. They are all very focused. And they all handle pressure very well. But in the time trial, Cadel was just as calm as he could be. I think I was more nervous than him. He'd had a glass of wine with us. He was talking with us, very normal, the next day he was very relaxed and very focused.

Hincapie said he has never felt prouder for any team he has ridden for than BMC, and believes they rode as close as possible to a perfect Tour:

When the negative things happened to us, it worked out in our favour. Losing the team time trial … had we won that, we might have burned some matches protecting yellow. Cadel having a technical glitch on the Télégraphe [climb on Friday's 19th stage]—he came back to us and we could protect him [while] the guys up the road, the Contadors and the Schlecks, killed themselves. We killed ourselves, but Cadel could stay with us.

Meanwhile, at the podium area Cadel had been taken to, the atmosphere was one of pandemonium—at best, organised chaos—as security attempted to limit access to the Tour winners. One party that is guaranteed access is French television, who took Cadel away to a small studio behind the podium to interview him for a live broadcast while all the teams began preparing for the traditional parade. Each team—with their sports directors and management—rides together up and down the Champs Elysées to thank the spectators for following their three-week ordeal, and to be championed by those spectators.

However, there was a delay with the interview, and there was concern that Cadel might miss his team's moment—they needed him riding with them in the yellow jersey.

As he was escorted down after the interview he was told he had 5 minutes, and was asked to do his drug test. Fortunately for Cadel, he is now used to drug tests, despite their intrusive nature—testers are required to observe the athlete's provision of a urine sample.

•   •   •

After the parade, Cadel finally got to return to a small boutique hotel that offered some privacy and was near the 950-room Concorde Lafayette, where most teams and race staff were staying. He arrived at about 7 pm, carrying his trophies, vases and Credit Lyonnaise lion, and with Chiara carrying the winner's bouquets in her arms.

Chiara had kissed Cadel on the Champs Elysées and, as if coming to terms with the fact that after all these years he had won the Tour, asked him 'What have you done?' as she gave him the Australian flag that he wore on the podium. But the couple had not had a private moment away from the public gaze all day. And they were not about to get one when they entered their hotel room to get ready for the evening celebrations at Le 1515.

Celebrations between riders, team staff and their partners and close friends had continued in the BMC bus on the 4-kilometre drive from the finish to the hotel; then after it stopped and Cadel stepped out, he was set upon by a woman trying to tear the jersey off his back for a charity.

Cadel and Chiara were in store for another surprise when they entered the hotel to find, waiting in the reception area, one of his oldest Australian friends. Martin Whitely was instrumental in helping Cadel during his formative years in mountain biking. It was a pleasant surprise for Cadel, who had spoken at length to Chiara about Whitely but had never got the chance to introduce him to her in person. The day he won the Tour seemed fitting.

The three shared a bottle of champagne before Cadel and Chiara showered and got dressed for the official BMC team party at Le 1515, which was attended by 300 people.

When Cadel was introduced at Le 1515 by BMC communications director Georges Luechinger as the new Tour champion, it was not lost on those present that Cadel's fortune had turned full circle. One year had passed since he was known as a long-time Tour contender who had once again fallen short of achieving his dream—he was even considered by many peers and observers to be way past his best, and unlikely to ever win the Tour. In 2010 Cadel had worn the yellow jersey for a day, and BMC was happy just because they'd participated in the Tour. When Cadel was introduced this time he was wearing the yellow jersey, and had an extra one to give to Andy Rihs—as well as the Toblerone Award.

The idea of the Toblerone Award came from Luechinger, who introduced it from his experience in football as a form of recognition, voted by an anonymous panel of team members, for the best player of the day; but at BMC it was changed to an award for the most valuable rider, not necessarily the rider with the best result. Cadel had won a few Toblerone Awards in his two seasons with BMC and suggested it should be given to the rider who did the 'most' in a day of racing—for example, the guy who spent most time riding into the wind. That way, the award—a giant block of Toblerone chocolate—could be shared throughout the team, with staff members being eligible for it on rest days on the grand tours.

Hence, come the Tour's finish in Paris and the celebration at Le 1515, the team felt there was no worthier recipient than the person who had financed the team and had the vision needed to support everyone on it. Andy Rihs could not conceal his delight at receiving the honour.

After giving Rihs the award, Cadel told his guests that the seed of his desire to win the Tour was planted when he was 14 years old and first saw coverage of the Tour on television. It was 1991, and Spaniard Miguel Indurain beat American Greg LeMond to win the first of his five titles. He said he thought to himself:

One day, it would be nice to ride that race, wouldn't it? Many years later, and many, many months, hours and years of hard work, here I am today. Having crossed the finish line on the Champs Elysées with this jersey is really something I can't quite believe.

After the festivities at Le 1515 finished, the merry BMC troupe returned to Cadel's hotel to drink a few more beers at the reception bar. Suddenly, after such a long day, hunger struck; and one of the group remembered that George Hincapie had yet to join them because he had gone to a nearby pizzeria to eat first. The call was put in to Hincapie to bring 10 takeaway pizzas to Cadel's hotel when he'd finished. Within half an hour the pizzas arrived; the team sat around drinking beer and eating pizza until about 5 o'clock in the morning

A few hours later, the day after the Tour finished, Cadel's plans were still uncertain. He had planned to return home to Stabio, Switzerland, for a short rest. He had also agreed to compete in two post-Tour criterium races. Other things that needed to be discussed included a mooted celebration visit to Australia, and suspending plans to race in the Vuelta a España from 20 August to 11 September. Lelangue said then that he wanted to give Cadel some space: 'For three days we will try not to phone each other. Then we will resume all calls and meetings and make the choice. But for the moment, let's celebrate the Tour de France.'

Lelangue said the major concern about racing the Vuelta so soon after the Tour de France was ensuring that the team— not just Cadel—had enough reserves to attempt a victory.

Racing both events is not new to Cadel. In 2009, after placing 29th in the Tour, he bounced back to take third place overall in the Vuelta. But no-one has won both races when they have been held in that order. In fact, only two riders have won both grand tours in the same year, and that was when the Vuelta was held before the Tour—Frenchmen Jacques Anquetil in 1963 and Bernard Hinault in 1978 both won the Tour five times.

Lelangue said then:

After what we have done since the beginning of the year—Tirreno, Catalunya, Romandy, Dauphiné, and all the success we have had in the Tour ... we will see if we have enough energy and power to go to the Vuelta. But if we go to the Vuelta it's to get a good result.

2011 TOUR DE FRANCE FINAL STANDINGS

General Classification—yellow jersey

1. Cadel Evans (BMC) at 86 hours 12 minutes 22 seconds
2. Andy Schleck (LeOpard) — 1 minute 34 seconds
3. Fränk Schleck (LeOpard) — 2 minutes 30 seconds
4. Thomas Voeckler (Europcar) — 3 minutes 20 seconds
5. Alberto Contador (Saxo Bank-Sungard) — 3 minutes 57 seconds
6. Samuel Sánchez (Euskaltel-Euskadi) — 4 minutes 55 seconds
7. Damiano Cunego (Lampre-ISD) — 6 minutes 5 seconds
8. Ivan Basso (Liquigas-Cannondale) — 7 minutes 23 seconds
9. Tom Danielson (Garmin-Cervélo) — 8 minutes 15 seconds
10. Jean-Christophe Péraud (Ag2r-La Mondiale) — 10 minutes 11 seconds

Points competition—green jersey

1. Mark Cavendish (HTC-Highroad) — 334 points
2. José Joaquin Rojas (Movistar) — 272 points
3. Philippe Gilbert (Omega Pharma-Lotto) — 236 points

King of the Mountains competition—polka dot jersey

1. Samuel Sánchez (Euskaltel-Euskadi) — 108 points
2. Andy Schleck (LeOpard) — 98 points
3. Jelle Vanendert (Omega Pharma-Lotto) — 74 points

Best Young Rider competition—white jersey

1. Pierre Rolland (Europcar) at 86 hours 23 minutes 5 seconds
2. Rein Taaramäe (Cofidis Le Crédit en Ligne) — 46 seconds
3. Jérôme Coppel (Saur-Sojasun) — 7 minutes 53 seconds

17

THE DAY AFTER ... AND DAYS AFTER

Cadel Evans woke up in Paris on Monday morning with only a few hours' sleep since his Tour de France win the day before. Sitting up until 5 am drinking beer and eating pizza was an extreme change in routine for a professional cyclist—but as Australia's first Tour winner, he had earned it.

But there was no time for Cadel to dwell on his achievement, and all that had happened in the previous 24 hours on that last day of the Tour; he and Chiara had to pack their bags and check out. Everything that morning was a rush. There were yellow jerseys, dirty clothes and things everywhere around the room—and everything had to be put in the suitcase. Once that was done they went down to breakfast; there were a few tired-looking faces among Cadel's teammates and their girlfriends and wives.

Cadel's Australian agent, Jason Bakker, was in the throng; his fatigue was not from celebrating his star client's success, but from handling the stream of media inquiries from Australia, where the final stage had been broadcast live into the early hours of the morning. Bakker, a former state representative cricket player who has a number of cyclists on his books—including Tasmanian Matt Goss who in March 2011 became the first Australian to win the Milan–San

Remo one-day classic in Italy—had not experienced a media response anything like the one he had just handled. Cadel's Tour victory was the lead item of all radio and television news bulletins in Australia. It was also the lead page-one story in most newspapers.

As dusty as Cadel might have felt, some decisions about his immediate future had to be made before he flew out from Paris that morning.

The first decision that was agreed upon concerned his proposed participation in the Vuelta a España: Cadel would not race it. He had wanted to do the Vuelta because his experience in 2009 had left a bad taste in his mouth, and because he wanted to get ready for the end of the year. But the Tour of Lombardy was so distant, and with the change in the calendar he had less time to recover, less time to repair—everything was against it.

But a trip to Australia was still on the cards, and one to the United States to end his season in the US Pro Challenge in Colorado. George Hincapie, through the whole Tour, kept suggesting that Cadel should go to Colorado. Cadel asked if it would be okay for the team if he went—because they'd left people like Greg Van Avermaet out of the Tour, and had riders like Santaromita, who didn't do the Giro so he could be fresh for the Vuelta.

Cadel's immediate plan was to return to his home in Stabio with his wife, Chiara. She and their friends who had come with her to Paris to watch the Tour finale were already booked on a budget flight with easyJet from Charles de Gaulle airport to Malpensa airport, near Milan, so Cadel opted to buy a ticket on the same flight and travel with her rather than take the flight already booked for him by the team. It seemed fitting that after travelling to the Tour start in Andy Rihs's private jet and then staying in a low-budget Campanille hotel for the Grand Départ as a Tour contender, he was leaving Paris on a low-budget carrier as the Tour champion after celebrating his historic win at a gala private function.

The scene at Charles de Gaulle kept Cadel's feet on the ground, too. A security officer attempted to confiscate his iPhone after he took a photo of himself with two members of the Australian women's track cycling team. And he found an insect in his sandwich, still alive and wrapped in plastic. At least it was fresh.

Also travelling with Cadel was Jason Bakker. While several days off awaited Cadel, there was still an endless list of media inquiries and sponsorship opportunities to consider, and plans for the visit to Australia to be locked in. Life had suddenly changed for Bakker, who had only signed Cadel in early 2010. He'd come to the Tour to see what it was all about and to have a bit of a holiday. You know you're busy when you have to recharge your iPhone twice in a day—Bakker had so many calls he had to recharge his four times in a day.

At Malpensa airport, Cadel, Chiara and Bakker walked into a phalanx of party balloons that had been blown up and hung by Chiara's parents and more friends—including his Italian physiotherapist Luca Ruiz, who drove the trio to the peace and quiet of Cadel and Chiara's home in Stabio.

Their arrival offered some respite from the whirlwind of attention. Cadel, Chiara and Bakker took the opportunity to eat at a local restaurant. After dinner and back in Stabio, it was time for Cadel to attend to more interviews with media in Australia, where a new day had dawned. A one-hour interview session arranged by Bakker had extended to one hour and 45 minutes when Cadel drew the line and said he needed to sleep.

The first thing that Cadel and Chiara did the day after returning to Stabio was to drive the 4 kilometres to visit Marina Sassi, the widow of Cadel's trainer Aldo, who died in December 2010 from a brain tumour. Then, with Sassi's daughter Valentina and her boyfriend, they visited Sassi's grave to place Cadel's Tour-winner's bouquet from the Champs Elysées and his race number there. As Cadel told the media:

> He would have been, I am sure, so, so proud of what we did— the way we raced, the way the race unfolded … of the whole effort … Andrea Morelli, my coach, now has taken up his role. So much of what we did was based on theories and mentality of what [Sassi] developed …

• • •

Cadel and Bakker spent most of the daylight hours in those first post-Tour days nutting out the rest of the season. Cadel and BMC had agreed that he could miss the Vuelta a España and instead race in the US Pro Challenge in Colorado, and travel beforehand to Australia for a victory parade of honour in Melbourne. But there was already a flood of sponsorship offers for Cadel and Bakker to consider, and invitations from organisers of the traditional post-Tour criteriums—one-hour races on a short, closed circuit that are designed to showcase the Tour stars in towns and cities around Europe where cycling fans may not have been able to see the Tour live. They are also lucrative for the rider, who will typically want to start in as many as he can.

Cadel is not a big fan of criteriums because of the fatigue he has felt and the need for him to recover and prepare for season-ending races. His position has been vindicated: in 2009, he missed the criteriums and placed third overall in the Vuelta a España and won the world championship.

In 2008, after he placed second in the Tour to Spaniard Carlos Sastre, he was due to attend a criterium in the Netherlands, but the night the Tour finished he injured his knee. The accident threatened his participation at the Beijing Olympics, and he had to withdraw.

However, after his 2011 Tour win, Cadel received an invitation via his European agent, Tony Rominger, from that same Dutch criterium organiser. Cadel was not about to be swayed by the money that he could command as the Tour champion. It is a lucrative block of racing for those who commit to it fully, though the amounts bandied about for appearances are far greater than what is really put on the table.

In 2011 Cadel agreed to race criteriums in Belgium and Germany after Rominger's insistence that 'the Tour winner every year is at these ones so to honour that tradition you should go'. As the Tour champion, it was no surprise that Cadel won the Sint-Niklaas criterium in Belgium.

The criteriums are not easy to race, considering most riders have not raced since the Tour; but victories like Cadel's win in Sint-Niklaas are more for the crowd than for a rider's career record, as they are primarily exhibition races.

Cadel's first appearance in the fabled yellow jersey in that Sint-Niklaas criterium on Friday 29 July, five days after the Tour, was almost a disaster, because he almost didn't have a yellow jersey to wear. When he arrived for the criterium, his spare yellow jersey from the Tour podium, which he had planned to wear, was not in his overnight bag. It was missing, and all he had was the unwashed one he wore as he raced onto the Champs Elysées, still adorned with his race number and dirty from his sweat. Cadel's predicament was averted thanks to Chris De Vos, the Belgian soigneur who was accompanying him, who had bought a yellow jersey for Cadel to one day sign. Alerted to the problem, De Vos quickly found it, ironed a BMC team patch onto its front and brought it with him for Cadel to race in. Of course, it wasn't Cadel's size, and it wasn't as body-hugging as it should've been, but it did the job.

For Cadel's next criterium, in Germany, teammate Steve Morabito's girlfriend came with a sewing kit and quickly improved the fit. As for the missing yellow jersey? It was later found in a bag of Cadel's that had found its way into another BMC team car in the mayhem of the Tour finish and was at the house of another soigneur, who had left home immediately after the Tour for a road trip.

Cadel travelled the next day, 30 July, from Belgium to Germany for the Sparkassen Giro Bochum Derny Race, a motor-paced criterium in which he finished second behind veteran Italian sprinter Alessandro Petacchi (Lampre-ISD). After the race, Cadel flew by helicopter to Zurich to appear on a Sunday television show the next day. Chiara met him there—he wanted her to share the novelty of a helicopter ride to the local football field behind their house in Stabio. When they arrived there was a little crowd. The town's policeman is a cycling fan, and opened the gates for them. Cadel apologised for the inconvenience on a Sunday night, but the policeman insisted that it was an honour.

There was little time to spare. A week later, on Tuesday 9 August, Cadel and Chiara were en route to Australia for his victory parade in Melbourne.

Cadel's trip to Australia was carefully planned, and it needed to be—there were multiple interests to balance: those of his BMC team, which wanted him to race in Colorado; those of the Victorian government, which had organised the parade and an evening civic reception; and his own eagerness to share his win with Australians.

The window of time was limited, considering that his trip to Australia meant he was travelling to Colorado the long way, and it would limit his time to adapt to the high altitude.

Not many teams would have allowed it, but BMC respected that Cadel is Australian. John Lelangue's words were, 'You deserve to celebrate it in Australia and your countrymen deserve to see you, so go there and enjoy it.

If you can get there in time for Colorado, great'. Cadel wanted to get there in time to prepare for Colorado and to ride a good race. That meant having time to train, and going somewhere quiet—it would have been healthier to go somewhere quiet and get life back to normal as soon as possible after the parade in Melbourne.

For that to happen, the parade needed to be held on Friday 12 August, even though the initial proposal was to stage it on Tuesday 16 August. That it actually fell into place was astounding.

Cadel, incredibly, feared that nobody would turn up for the parade. He was quickly reassured that he had no reason to fear a lack of public interest in his trip: he was welcomed at the airport by Victorian Premier Ted Baillieu, and there were giant placards on the roadside championing his success.

Cadel was met with a wave of adoration in Australia—people were thrilled about his win and by his willingness to share his spectacular feat with them.

There was still plenty of speculation about how many people would turn up for the parade, in which Cadel rode in a yellow jersey—on the yellow bike that he didn't wish to ride on the last stage of the Tour—with a group of 20 children in red 'Team Cadel' T-shirts riding behind him. As it happened, it was televised live by all the Australian networks, and was attended by an estimated 30,000 people over a 1-kilometre route that finished in Federation Square. There were people wearing yellow as far as the eye could see—yellow hair-ribbons and yellow socks and yellow

T-shirts. Newsreaders wore yellow ties. In riding the yellow BMC bike, Cadel probably gave BMC more brand exposure than if he had taken it to a bike show.

Cadel was still surprised by the turnout in Melbourne: it was likened to the welcome home that was arranged for Aboriginal boxing champion Lionel Rose in 1964 after he returned from winning his world title in Japan and was taken in an open car through crowds of cheering supporters to Melbourne Town Hall. Otherwise, nobody had seen anything like it—even in a sporting hub like Melbourne. Cadel's win was likened in Australia to that of *Australia II* in the 1983 America's Cup.

Cadel's popularity even surpassed that of American talk-show star Oprah Winfrey when she visited Melbourne during her highly publicised national tour of Australia in early 2011. Oprah attracted 8000 people to her public appearance at Federation Square. Cadel openly hoped that his feat—being the first Australian to win the Tour de France—would pull a greater crowd than Oprah.

'I was kind of surprised when I landed in Australia and saw my picture on the front page of the paper. I'm just so happy people appreciated it and people do it. I am here to enjoy it', Cadel said.

Cadel also shared the reasons he loves cycling. It is not just the thrill of competition, preparation and producing the best possible result. He certainly has never sought the fame and the trappings that come with being one of the world's best cyclists. Asked after his parade what he loves about the sport, he said:

A lot of it … feeling good, going fast. That would be the main part of it. It's that feeling of being on your bike … the road is there and it might be a long thin ribbon of asphalt uphill if you are feeling good, downhill if you are feeling fast … there's the noise, the wind in your hair and the freedom of it. When you are having a bad day, that's where our sport can be a little unforgiving. When you are feeling good, it's not that hard, but when you are having a bad day in the third week of a grand tour in the mountains and you have got to be there— in 2008 when I had my crash, that was the hardest race I did in my life—when you are 5 or 10 per cent off and you are there fighting for the win, or your place on GC, it's hours and hours of suffering …

In the same interview, Cadel elaborated on what has driven him to get where he is, and still hopes to be in years to come:

In sport, or any walk of life, [people] have this drive. People week after week, day after day, month after month have this constant drive to keep going and succeeding or improving … That is what makes people really successful in whatever their chosen endeavour is. I love the sport. I love racing. I wanted to see how good I could be. From an early age I wanted to give everything I could to the sport, so that when I retire I could say I did everything I could. I don't want to have regrets … To be a professional—first, it was a dream, and then it became an opportunity. I never want to waste that opportunity. I want to keep it like that because to do something you love as a profession is something a lot of people strive for, but can't make happen.

Cadel doesn't think highly of social commentators. Before he had even returned to Australia he had learned of the remarks by one woman in Australia who earns her living commentating on social issues and had spoken out against the public adoration for Cadel's victory.

Mia Freedman, who has a website and writes a Sunday newspaper column, appeared on Channel Nine's *Today Show* in Australia on the Monday after Cadel's win. She questioned the praise he was attracting, surmising that he had not contributed to any improvement in Australian society by winning a bike race, and complained that Australian sports stars get far too much credit for their feats compared to medical, theatrical and scientific achievers. She ignored—or didn't not know about—Cadel's background as a long-time supporter of a free Tibet, his sponsorship of a Tibetan child and his commitment to a number of charities.

Cadel has never placed sporting achievements above those in other fields of life. But it would only be natural for someone like him to take offence at Freedman's remarks, especially as she had the chance to clarify them in her Sunday newspaper column. Instead she spoke only of her 'week from hell' after the vitriol that came her way, and her presumption that 'from everything I now know about Cadel Evans, I think he's the kind of humble person who'd be the first to agree [with me]'.

• • •

The inevitable downside of Cadel's trip to Australia was the time that was taken from training. Not that he planned for a lot of training, but he had hoped to fit in an hour in each of his four days in Australia riding his bike on the indoor rollers in the penthouse suite of the Crown Casino. In the midst of the enormous demands on his time, that expectation turned out to be unrealistic.

Amid the organised chaos of each day, Cadel was visited by his mother, Helen, grandmother, Gwen Cocks, and Damien Grundy, his former mountain bike coach. They all also attended the civic reception held on the night of his victory parade, which was a who's who of Victorian political and sporting personalities.

Cadel did get the chance to relax when he, Chiara, his mother and grandmother ate together at his favourite Melbourne restaurant, Syracuse, where he had celebrated his 21st birthday 13 years earlier. The dinner was so enjoyable that he went back there the next night with Grundy.

Outside of attending the parade and various receptions and conducting media interviews, Cadel's time was taken up with meetings over sponsorship opportunities. But riders are limited by their trade-team contracts as to how many of those opportunities they can seize.

Bike riders need to be a member of a team. They sell their image to the team, and the team owns it. That's to a rider's advantage when they don't have many opportunities for sponsorship—but when they go to the Tour it's a bit of a disadvantage, because there are many offers they can't accept. Every company associated with a team that wins has used it to their advantage.

It's understandable that investors in a team would command such control of a rider's image. Andy Rihs, for example, invested for six or seven years in building up the BMC team to go to and win the Tour de France. Jim Ochowicz had the vision to build up a team—to start small, get bigger and by 2011 start in the Tour—but it was always Rihs who backed it financially. Whichever way you want to look at it, he'd been there to back the team and then, when it finally achieved more than was reasonably hoped for, other people suddenly wanted to take advantage of it.

Rihs's investment in Cadel has been substantial. He's been behind Cadel since the end of 2009, when he broke his contract with Omega Pharma-Lotto in November that year. He paid Cadel for that November and December; he's backed him ever since, and then, after Cadel crossed the finish line in Grenoble, other people stepped in and tried to profit from it.

One of the important post-Tour issues for a team and their leader to address is the allocation of bonuses to riders and the staff. Cadel's €450,000 for winning the Tour overall went into the team kitty along with every Euro won in their overall and stage placings, and in intermediate sprints and various classifications. The general policy is for the grand total to be split amongst everyone, with riders getting a certain percentage and staff another.

For Cadel, the financial wealth from a Tour win represents contractual clout, and soon after the Tour it was announced that he had re-signed with BMC to the end of 2014. However, he was also due a financial bonus for his victory. That was to be a fee paid to him from insurance that was based on the likelihood of him winning the Tour before it began.

There's a wait for the overall winner, pending the final outcome of all doping tests taken during the Tour. As for Cadel's teammates, besides their share of prize money, it is common practice for them to receive something from their leader in return for their work to help him win. Some Tour winners give teammates financial bonuses or gifts of all kinds. After the 2011 Tour, Cadel gave each BMC rider on the Tour a fully paid holiday for their family.

The deal for Cadel's eight teammates was that they could take a business-class trip to anywhere and for any length of time—so long as they were ready and fit to race in 2012. All they had to do was book the trip through Cadel's travel agent, Troy, who is based in Hong Kong. Cadel also said they had to send him a postcard, because he had no time to go anywhere.

Of course Cadel did go to Australia, and while he was there, he and Chiara spent a week with Ivan Santaromita at Hamilton Island in Queensland.

Of the team staff, one member received a special reward—Cadel's osteopath David Bombeke has always dreamed of owning a particular kind of watch. Cadel gave him one, inscribed with the words: 'Tour de France 2011. We did it.'

• • •

When Cadel warned that he would be slightly lacking form to challenge for overall victory in the US Pro Challenge in Colorado, he wasn't bluffing. Having trained and raced at high altitude often as a mountain biker and as a road racer, he knew the demands that such conditions place on a rider, and what is needed to be at optimal level. This was the first time he had done a stage race at altitude; if he'd had more time to train at altitude, it is probable that his result would have been better.

It was no coincidence that all the top finishers had raced the Tour of Utah from 9 to 14 August. Anyone not from Colorado would notice the change in altitude walking up the glacier Mont Blanc. When riders are climbing it flat out, a 2, 3 or 5 per cent difference becomes very obvious. Nevertheless, Cadel's seventh place at 1 minute 18 seconds to American winner Levi Leipheimer (RadioShack) was still a creditable result.

Most important for Cadel, though, was that he arrived several days before the race started on 22 August—and in time to see the last stage of the Tour of Utah finish. After all the hype and hoopla of his Australian visit—and so soon after the Tour—he needed several days of riding alone, to clear his head as much as to adapt to the new conditions. At training camps Cadel has the opportunity to focus on riding his bike and catch up on being a human being—to relax and reflect.

One outcome from the US Pro Challenge was that it led

to Cadel and Andy Schleck getting a chance to share 'that beer' the pair spoke about on the night of the Tour time trial in Grenoble when the Luxembourger telephoned to congratulate Cadel on his Tour win. The catalyst was BMC sports director Mike Sayer, a former rider, urging Cadel after one stage to support the race sponsor by sampling a beer in a nearby bar. Sayer says:

> He was in a fantastic mood and really very relaxed. I am a huge fan of the New Belgium Brewery out of Fort Collins [Colorado], and I felt it was my obligation to introduce the yellow jersey to a company that gives a lot of support to cycling in the USA. Most of the time, we would have a beer at dinner while we were all sitting, relaxing and chatting. It was really nice to see Cadel so relaxed after all the pressure he was under prior to the Tour.

Cadel joined Sayer for a beer, and George Hincapie and several other BMC riders were encouraged to join them when they crossed paths on the way down. Soon after, Andy and Fränk Schleck suddenly entered, prompting Cadel to invite them to join him for a drink.

It was the eve of the hardest day of the US Pro Challenge, the 220-kilometre stage 2 from Gunnison to Aspen, but that didn't curb Cadel's spontaneity or Schleck's willingness to accept the invitation. They sat there together and drank to each other's health.

Schleck's respect for Cadel grew in the 2011 Tour. During the Tour of Oman in February 2012 he said:

The years before there was always a day where he cracked, where he was weak. He didn't have that [in 2011] because he was really confident. He was really calm. He didn't stress himself. Even when I was out there with 4½ minutes [on stage 19 to Galibier Serre-Chevalier] he took the race in his hands.

Even though Cadel left the bar before the Schlecks, his suffering the next day began on the first climb, where he followed American Tom Danielson, a strong climber from the area who knew the climbs well. Cadel hung back with Danielson, but ultimately they fell off the pace and were dropped. Afterwards, when the next couple of groups came back, Fränk went up to Cadel and said, 'Oh man … I knew I shouldn't have had that last mojito'.

Cadel's suffering may not have been exactly Fränk Schleck's … but as he rode on to the finish, he knew, too, that his racing for the season was over.

18

THE DEFENCE AND NEW CHALLENGES

On the eve of the 2012 Tour de France route presentation in Paris on 18 October 2011, Cadel Evans met Andy Rihs, Jim Ochowicz, John Lelangue and George Hincapie for dinner in a restaurant that now symbolises the way their shared dream of winning the Tour became a reality.

The five had eaten at the Italian restaurant near the Champs Elysées on the night before the 2011 Tour route was unveiled and, as they did this time, they posed for a group photo in front of the nearby Arc du Triomphe as they walked back to their hotel afterwards.

Lelangue recalls how the five looked on to the Champs Elysées while posing for the photo in October 2010 and pledged that they would be back there in July; a year and three months after Cadel's Tour win they were able to say they'd done it.

However, despite the historic significance of Cadel becoming the first Australian to win the Tour de France, and the fact that his success came after seven attempts—including two runner-up finishes with deficits that were less than a minute—winning the Tour in 2012 will pose a far bigger challenge than winning it the first time. Lelangue takes a pragmatic view:

For me it doesn't change anything, except that now everybody's considering Cadel as the defending champion. Until now we were the underdogs and that was fine. But we still took all responsibility. So … there is no problem changing. We are going with Cadel and to the same race, with the same objective. For the team, it doesn't change anything.

However, no two Tours de France are exactly the same, especially for the reigning champion, which is just as Cadel expected when preparing for his first defence in 2012.

His self-belief and attention to detail was as strong as ever, and his pre-Tour race program was more or less the same; but it was evident, as soon as he sat down in October to strategise the season ahead with his existing and new BMC teammates and management, that the dynamics would change.

As Cadel told journalists after his victory parade in Melbourne:

When you are painted up as the favourite everyone is looking at you. And now for 2012 we have to build a completely different team, completely different tactics. Everyone is going to be watching us to control the race—maybe not from start to finish but for a good part of it. That building process started six months ago.

Come 30 June and the 2012 Tour start in the Belgian city of Liège, Cadel would no longer be underestimated—and neither would his BMC team, which had surprised many sceptics in 2011 and been strengthened for 2012 with the recruitment of several important riders. They included former world champion Thor Hushovd of Norway, the 2011 world number one–ranked Philippe Gilbert of Belgium, two young and up-and-coming climbers in Tejay van Garderen of the United States and Steve Cummings from Great Britain, and the seasoned Italian time-triallist Marco Pinotti.

Adding to the changing landscape of the Tour was that Cadel's main rival, 26-year-old Andy Schleck, was likely to come back wiser after an extra year's experience after racing under a new sports director, Belgian Johan Bruyneel. Bruyneel steered American Lance Armstrong to seven Tour wins, and Spaniard Alberto Contador to two titles. He offers Andy a lot of experience, having been there and seen so much of the detail behind past Tour wins.

There is also the advantage Schleck may get from having his brother, Fränk, race with him. Does one's brother make a more committed domestique? The answer isn't clear, but Cadel certainly has a lot of experience with the two-up brotherly attack.

Also likely to be stronger opponents for Cadel are the other contenders who placed behind him—and riders like Briton Bradley Wiggins, whose chances in 2011 were cruelled by crashes and injury. On paper, the 2012 Tour de France looks well suited to Wiggins. There are always five or six contenders, and if those two or three don't deliver, there will be two or three outsiders who really do something extraordinary. Tony Martin won't automatically become a contender by virtue of having won the time trial at the world championships, but he's a rider with talent and depth and is someone who might come into it.

On paper, someone like Andreas Klöden is good, but it's been a few years since he's done well in a solid three-week race, and it's unclear whether he wants to go for it or just be there for Schleck. Levi Leipheimer will also be one to watch for. He should be on his own at Omega Pharma-Lotto, but Martin will be there too, as will Italian Vincenzo Nibali (Liquigas), who placed third in the Giro d'Italia in 2010 and went on to win the Vuelta a España the same year.

One of the most interesting threats could come from France—not from Thomas Voeckler, but from his teammate Pierre Rolland, pending the development in his time-trial-ling. After his performance in 2011 it's unlikely the peloton will let Voeckler go. He was very good in the time trial; he's still developing and improving, so even if he doesn't get that bonus 2 or 3 minutes, he can still be there among the contenders. But some observers doubt he'll be a threat for the win.

Rolland has got to be thinking of himself—and that comes down to the capabilities of the Europcar team, the qualities of the individual characters, the riders, and also which man steps up when there are two good riders in a team.

As he prepared for 2012, Cadel also had to consider the impact of Spaniard Alejandro Valverde's return from a two-year suspension for breaching anti-doping laws. Another consideration was the absence of Contador should the Court of Arbitration for Sport (CAS) accept an appeal against the Spanish cycling federation's February 2011 ruling that cleared him after he tested positive for the illegal drug clenbuterol in the 2010 Tour. Contador's absence was confirmed in February 2012 when CAS ruled that Contador be banned for two years retroactively—a finding that would sideline him until 5 August 2012.

There was also the matter of a different Tour route. When the 2012 route was leaked online a few days before the official presentation at the Palais des Congrés in Paris on Tuesday 18 October, Cadel refrained from making any judgement on the course until he saw it officially unveiled and knew that it was correct. He had read all the reports about the leaked route, but didn't look at the map on Google Earth; knowing the route a week earlier wouldn't make any difference.

When Tour director Christian Prudhomme unveiled the 3489-kilometre route for the 2012 race, Cadel liked what he saw. While there are only three summit finishes, many felt the route was harder than it appeared, with 25 climbs as opposed to 23 in 2011. It also includes a 6.1-kilometre prologue time-trial and 20 stages: nine are flat, four are in mid-level mountains, five are in high mountains, and two are time trials. The two time trials—38 kilometres on stage 9 and 52 kilometres on stage 19—make for a total of 96 kilometres in time-trialling, later increased to 100 kilometres due to a tweak in one of the time-trial courses.

The clockwise route passes the Vosges and Jura mountains before entering the Alps for two days, then heads south, then to the south-west towards the Pyrenees for three days, and then north to the Tour finish in Paris. The first 10 days of the 2012 Tour are a real mix of everything—there is a mountain-top finish (stage 7) and a big time trial as well (stage 9).

So happy was Cadel about the route that, in an interview with the *Sydney Morning Herald*, he said he even looked forward to his team being labelled as 'favourites' rather than as underdogs or outsiders. He went on to say:

> It is like a modern Tour for the first half, and a historic Tour for the second half—half and half means it's more for a good, all-round, consistent rider.

Asked about the strength of his team, which has been bolstered by the recruitment of Belgian Philippe Gilbert, Norwegian Thor Hushovd, American Tejay van Garderen, Briton Steve Cummings and Italian Marco Pinotti, Cadel said:

> You would sort of hope we go there as favourites. Who knows what the attitude towards us will be in 2012, but it's going to be a different type of race for us. We are going to have to improvise on a different style of racing and it's on a different course. The team for 2011 was great and obviously we did the job that we had to do. But I am really happy. The acquisition of guys like Gilbert and Hushovd is good, but [having] Tejay and Steven Cummings for the mountains is also going to be important.

The Tour route launch, which included a superbly edited highlights video of Cadel's win, was also attended by his key rivals for the title, Andy and Fränk Schleck and Spain's triple winner Alberto Contador, who had then still hoped to be available to race the Tour. And the occasion was not lost on Cadel:

> I looked at the town names, but I'm now anxious to see the course. I'd rather wait here and see the nice film and see it officially in good detail. Ninety-six kilometres of time-trialling is favourable, but in the race we'll see [how favourable it] will be.

• • •

Cadel and BMC learned from what they did for 2011—they came away with a result and with confidence. But it's going to be a completely different race in 2012, and there will be a different approach. At a meeting in October, one thing that Cadel, along with trainer Andrea Morelli and BMC team president Jim Ochowicz, decided would be as similar as possible is Cadel's build-up to the Tour.

Cadel had never before faced a new season being able to say that he would like to emulate the build-up of the previous season. Some years he had fared well, but there had been inconsistencies and internal team issues. But after 2011 he felt totally satisfied with what he had achieved and, importantly, excited and confident about riding in the coming season as a Tour champion.

One thing that needed to be taken into account in planning for the year was the adjustment that comes with impending parenthood: Cadel and his wife, Chiara, had plans to adopt a child. It had been a two-year process and in October they were awaiting final confirmation. In December 2011 they flew to Ethiopia to meet their little boy and, by January 2012, 15-month-old Robel was living with them in Stabio. Understandably, the responsibilities that come with parenthood required change from Cadel and Chiara, and that, in turn, was to have an impact on his cycling.

Cadel quickly took to fatherhood. He believes it has helped him grow as a person, and that the presence of Robel has been as beneficial to him and Chiara as the opportunity of being raised in a loving family should prove to be for Robel, who was found by police abandoned in a cardboard box by the side of the road.

After being told that their application to adopt had been approved and rushing to Ethiopia from Australia, Cadel and Chiara first met Robel on Christmas Day. The adoption process was through the non-profit organisation Pro Etiopia-Infanzia, which facilitates adoptions between Switzerland and Ethiopia. For Cadel and Chiara, getting that final approval was the end of a very long process. It began in 2009 when they first applied, through 2010 when they underwent suitability tests, and in 2011 they completed reams of paperwork and waited for the telephone call telling them they could fly to Ethiopia and spend time with their prospective adopted child.

In between training, racing and sponsorship commit-ments, Cadel spends every minute he can with Robel, as he told the media before heading off for a training camp in the Sierra Nevada in southern Spain in early May:

> Being a family now ... we are more than happy. It's one thing being a couple, and another thing having a kid. Molly [the family dog] is in there too ... the poor thing. She gets her tail and ears pulled. But she is very good about it. It's been incredible, that's for sure. I appreciate being at home more now. He comes to visit me at a few races, which is always nice. He is growing a lot, learning a lot and changing quickly, developing quickly.
>
> Most of all I appreciate my time at home. At home, I spend time either on my bike or with him. I used to waste time doing other stuff, but now I spend it with him. It's so relaxing being with him, watching him grow and learn.

When asked what has stood out the most in his first six months of being a father, Cadel said:

> A friend told me that it's amazing what you learn about yourself from your children. Seeing him learn every day, I am learning from him as well. That's probably the thing that has surprised me the most. He copies everything I do. Everything I do, he does. That makes me behave myself a bit better.

In 2012 Cadel's focus is his family and the Tour in July; he can't accept anything that compromises his performance at the Tour, other than family-related things.

Late in 2011 and into early 2012, Cadel had been under increasing pressure from an adoring Australian public, sponsors and race organisers, to spend more time back in Australia than he'd planned, to race the Tour Down Under in Adelaide in January—an event that he last competed in 2010 and, after missing it in 2011, was reluctant to return to for fear of compromising his Tour defence.

There was some discussion about just visiting the Tour Down Under, but eliminating trips clears space for Cadel to prepare for the Tour. As much as he would have liked to have been there for Australian cycling, for Cadel it's black and white: all professional decisions this year are informed by their probable impact on his Tour defence. It's a firm and hard philosophy, but it's the philosophy he has to have to win the Tour.

And there was certainly no possibility of Cadel considering the Giro, as much as he would still like to race it and go for the win before he finally retires. He learned in 2010 how difficult it is to race the Tour after the Giro—and Contador's difficulties after winning the Giro in 2011 and finishing fifth in the Tour was a reminder of that. And, as Lelangue says, the specificity required in preparing for a grand tour is now too great to accommodate both: 'When you do the Giro in May you have to prepare, but then you can't do your Tour reconnaissance in May, or your altitude training for the Tour.'

Being one of the top world tour teams—in light of its win in 2011, strong off-season recruitment and its proven ability to race as a unit—means there will be a far greater expectation that BMC will assume greater responsibility in the Tour.

They knew they had to be prepared to take more responsibility in certain moments in the race, and that's where the recruitment got complicated—the question there being the type of rider they would recruit.

Much attention had been placed on the perceived dangers of recruiting stars like Hushovd and Gilbert and whether or not they would be totally committed to riding for Cadel. Many observers did not realise how far back talks about signing up a pure sprinter had gone, nor that when Hushovd was announced as the first among the two new stars to join, that he was not seen as such a sprinter. He has won bunch sprints at the Tour, but he seems to be changing as a rider. He's now a strong all-rounder, and his results in 2011 show that.

Hushovd is a talented rider who is also capable of winning stages, but at BMC he will also be focusing on the classics. There is no team time trial in the Tour, but he's a great, strong, reliable, experienced rider to have.

BMC's plans to sign Hushovd and Gilbert were aimed at taking pressure off Cadel to win early in 2012. It was planned that Hushovd's goal would be the Tour of Flanders and Paris–Roubaix classics, while Gilbert's would be the hilly Flèche-Wallonne and Liège–Bastogne–Liège classics in Belgium, and the Dutch Amstel Gold Race, in which Cadel would race to help Gilbert.

The plan then was for Hushovd and Gilbert to support Cadel in the Tour, with any stage-winning opportunities sought so long as they do not compromise Cadel's race—either tactically, or by demanding they expend too much energy that could otherwise be used to serve Cadel's interests.

When it comes to overall recruitment, there is an element of lining up your ducks—and that is not altogether simple.

Teams have to start planning a long way in advance to sign the big riders, and there's team budgeting to consider. A team may have signed riders for two or three years who they hope will do something, but who are perhaps not living up to expectations. They may need to bring in others that will fill that gap, but not all the good climbers are free at any given time—of the 10 best in the world, only two are free every year.

There are other criteria a potential recruit needs to fulfil: Do they want to be in the team that's recruiting? What sort of personality do they have? Will they fit? Some riders are in talks for two or three years and the negotiations don't come to fruition.

BMC needed a group that could be strong in the mountains. It is an American team—and there are American riders with a lot of potential, like Tejay van Garderen, who they signed. Van Garderen is one of BMC's top acquisitions for the short and long term, and they first spoke to him about joining BMC during the Tour, even though he was unsure if he would switch. Van Garderen is a racer who has demonstrated his guile in seizing opportunities when they arise, such as on the stage 8 to Super-Besse Sancy where Hushovd defended his yellow jersey.

Insiders expect that van Garderen will be there for the Dauphiné and Switzerland races in the future, and Colorado, if not becoming a grand tour rider. Whether he will be a contender or possible winner, it's probably a bit early to tell. The main thing is that he is someone who has all the capabilities—he just doesn't have experience, and he wants to learn. If he races for Cadel's interests, Cadel will be able to help him learn and put him in the right direction in four years if he wants to go and try for the general classification at the Tour.

Gilbert and Cadel have been teammates before, and the two are friends. The bond with Gilbert is real, as was shown by Cadel's assistance in his first races as world champion in 2009 to help Gilbert win the Classica Sabatini and Tour of Lombardy races.

The one stage where Cadel won't have total commitment from the whole team in the 2012 Tour is the finish in Liège [stage 1]. Normally that wouldn't be tolerated, but an exception will be made for Gilbert. However, if he gets the yellow jersey it is unlikely the team will stay on the front for him to defend it—it also depends on which sprinters are there.

An important factor in its programming is that BMC will not just work towards ensuring Cadel starts the Tour fresh, but that all of the nine riders selected for the race do.

John Lelangue's plan before the season began was for a long-list of 14 riders from his 26-strong roster to have a race program designed to 'preserve them and make sure everything is done so that if they race the Tour, even if they jump in at the last moment, that they are totally fresh to help Cadel'.

Strengthening the team means that some of those who rode with him to victory in 2011 may miss out in 2012. While

BMC's depth is a plus, telling someone who really deserves to be there that they have to stay home will be hard.

Belgian teammate Greg Van Avermaet—who went on to win the Paris–Tours classic in October after narrowly missing out on a Tour berth in 2011—is an example of how well those who do miss out can respond and even use the opportunities that come to further their own professional careers. He managed it very well, knowing that if he didn't ride the 2011 Tour, he had more for the Vuelta and the world titles.

The flip side for those riders who are told they won't be riding with Cadel in the Tour is that they are granted opportunities to lead the team in other races, such as the Giro d'Italia, which Cadel again decided to omit from his schedule.

Pending injury and condition, there is a core to the BMC team that ideally will be there at the Tour start line in Liège for his title defence. They include George Hincapie, Marcus Burghardt, Steve Morabito, Micki Schär and Brent Bookwalter. With Cadel, that makes for six riders. They hold their places because of the strength and commitment they have shown Cadel since he joined BMC and raced with them in the 2010 Tour.

That leaves only three places for the likes of Hushovd, Gilbert, van Garderen, Quinziato, Pinotti, Santaromita and Greg Van Avermaet. It will be a tough decision.

●　●　●

Cadel's 2012 season began slightly differently than first planned. It started in the first of four races in the Mallorca

Challenge in Spain. But then he resumed racing as originally planned two weeks later in the GP Città di Lugano Trophy one-day race in Italy on 26 February. Much of February 2011 was spent moving from the apartment he and Chiara rented in Stabio to a house nestled off the main street behind a row of trees.

After the GP Città di Lugano, Cadel's race program almost mirrored his 2011 schedule, with the Strade Bianche on 3 March and the Tirreno–Adriatico stage race from 7 to 14 March in Italy. The rest of his build-up to the Tour de France was to include the Critérium International in France (24 March); the Amstel Gold Race in the Netherlands (15 April); the Flèche-Wallonne (18 April) and Liège–Bastogne–Liège (22 April) classics in the Belgian Ardennes; the Tour de Romandie (24–29 April) in Switzerland; and the Critérium du Dauphiné in France (3–10 June), with training camps interspersed.

Cadel missed the Ardennes in 2011 through a knee injury, but wanted to reintroduce those races—to be there for Gilbert and get in some one-day races to prepare for the different mindset for the Olympic Games in London and the world championships in Limburg.

Cadel's other tweak was omitting the Volta a Catalunya soon after the Tirreno–Adriatico. Because of his efforts in Tirreno in 2011, Cadel started the Spanish tour, in which he placed eighth overall, feeling flat.

However, apart from winning the three-stage Critérium International in fine fashion, the European Spring turned into a problematic one for Cadel, who had health issues. By the time the spring classics had passed, neither Hushovd nor Gilbert had won a classic. Meanwhile, Cadel was battling a sinus infection that saw him abandon the Amstel Gold Race and then skip the Flèche-Wallonne and Liège–Bastogne–Liège classics in the Belgian Ardennes before returning to race in the Tour de Romandie in Switzerland.

Cadel's return to the Tour de Romandie was not like it was in 2011, when he won the race overall, but he did ride much better than he had in the Amstel Gold Race and was reassured that he was on track for an ideal build-up to the Tour and his title defence.

After the Tour de Romandie, Cadel spent two and half days on reconnaissance of some of the Tour stages nearby, and by the time he was driving back to his home in Stabio, he was in good spirits, knowing that he could throw himself into the final weeks leading up to his next race, the Critérium du Dauphiné, as enthusiastically as ever. 'Everything stays the same', Cadel was reported as saying.

Cadel has reason to be confident. He rode strongly in the Tour de Romandie, especially on the penultimate stage in the mountains, where he was eighth; even if his poor results in the opening and closing time trials, in which he finished 80th and 40th respectively en route to placing 29th overall at 2 minutes 7 seconds to Bradley Wiggins, confirmed the reality that his Tour-winning form was still some way off:

I didn't get to Romandy at the level I wanted, especially with the No. 1 on my back. I had to take a different mindset: look at it to get better and test myself to see where I was. Obviously, I was a long way from the front, but I have been improving, and that's the most important thing right now.

Asked how heartening his eighth place in the mountain stage—won by Spaniard Luis Leon Sánchez (Rabobank)—was, Cadel replied:

> I was getting better every day. We were looking at my numbers [wattage and heart rates]. I was there, but I wasn't feeling I could do a good sprint, to try and give Sánchez a good run, which I think at my normal level I would at least have been able to give him. But [the form] is improving. Going from bad to a lot less bad is a bit behind what I am used to at the Tour de Romandie. But that's okay … in terms of July, it might not even be a bad thing at all.

Cadel certainly wasn't bluffing, nor—as some suspected—was he deliberately trying to tweak his build-up to peak condition to coincide with the last 10 days of the Tour (which ends on 22 July) and remain for the Olympic Games a week later and the world titles from 15 to 23 September:

> No … My first goal of the year is the Tour, and you have to be good for the first 10 days of the Tour. So that's always been my goal, and then I will start to think about the Olympics. I was always more looking at the second half of the year than the first, but when things still didn't come together like they did last year—because I didn't win Tirreno–Adriatico, because

I didn't win Romandy—people were paying a little bit more attention.

When Cadel was asked about Wiggins and his contrasting pathway towards the Tour—he won the Paris–Nice and Tour de Romandie events—Cadel spoke of Wiggins' Sky team rather than about the individual. He understands the benefits of having a rock-solid, committed team behind him, and said: 'They'll go into the Tour more convinced than they may otherwise have been. Last year, winning the way I did in Tirreno helped in that regard.'

Cadel knows, better than most Tour contenders, just how crucial a team's belief is: 'My teammates know that I can win the Tour. People know that I can win the Tour.'

•   •   •

Despite the Tour's importance, there was no downplaying the significance Cadel placed on the Olympics and world titles when he planned the year. The schedule makes for a demanding second half of the season; hence the tempered first half is designed to help him keep the reserves to handle it.

The absence of a team time trial in the 2012 Tour provided four extra days for training or to conduct reconnaissance of other routes in the race.

Because of the Olympics and world titles, Cadel had considered starting the season even later than he did—in March at the Volta a Catalunya in Spain—to make sure he had greater reserves. But he loves Tirreno–Adriatico and was excited about racing as the defending champion. He also has strong ties to Italy, especially after the death of his trainer Aldo Sassi. During the 2010 race, Cadel telephoned Sassi, who told him he had a headache and felt terrible. When Cadel called the next day, Sassi had returned home still complaining of the same symptoms. Later that week he was in a specialist hospital in Milan for surgery to remove a tumour. Sassi's drive to work with Cadel continued to almost his last breath and included attending the 2010 world road titles in Geelong.

•   •   •

Cadel is not perturbed by the proximity of the Olympic Games to the Tour finish on 22 July. The men's road race is on the Saturday after the Tour finishes, followed by the time trial two days later—both events that Cadel is a candidate for selection in. There is one adjustment Cadel will make come the Tour's finish: win, draw or lose, he won't be staying until five o'clock in the morning drinking beer and eating pizza.

Cadel has raced in three Olympic Games—in 1996 at Atlanta and in 2000 at Sydney—as a member of Australia's cross-country mountain bike team, where he placed ninth and seventh respectively; then in 2008 at Beijing in the road race and time-trial events, where he finished 16th and fifth respectively.

The Tour de France and the Olympics are both fantastic sporting events, but there are some distinct differences between the two.

At the Olympics there are constraints on who you can and can't talk to, and what you can and can't talk about. Cadel found that out firsthand in 2008, when he was told that he could not comment during the Games in Beijing on his views on a free Tibet. It's a cause that he supports— and he demonstrated so in races leading up to that year's Tour by exposing a Free Tibet undershirt while racing in Europe.

The Tour makes no restriction on the free expression of thought by the riders—and as an organisation is generally willing to listen and respond to their concerns.

Another difference between the two events is that riders go to the Tour with people they know well—other riders, and experienced staff who know their job and what the riders do. Athletes go to the Olympics with people they've never met or seen. They go from a familiar environment where they know everyone, to the Olympics, where somebody they've never met rubs their legs and fixes their bike.

Cadel does not know Matt White—one of the national selectors and a head sports director on the Australian Orica-GreenEDGE team—very well. And considering the candidacy of so many riders on Orica-GreenEDGE for the five-man Olympic road race, it was seen as important that Cycling Australia appoint an independent voice among the selectors on the panel, to ensure no conflict of interest arises with Olympic selection. Early in 2012 Allan Peiper, who has the same role as White on the American Garmin-Barracuda team, was added to the Australian selection panel, which now numbers five.

Cadel's eagerness to ride for Australia—and to do all he can to help an Australian win, even if it is not him—is rock solid. White says that when he sent his first email to all Olympic candidates to gauge riders' interest in attending the first Games briefing, Cadel was the first to respond— he did so in about 30 minutes.

As well as his Tour experience, helping Cadel in the selection process was his strength in the time trial, with Australia having qualified for two spots and both entrants having to come from the road team.

• • •

When Cadel won the 2011 Tour de France it was a big breakthrough, but defending the title is likely to be harder than winning it the first time.

What is certain is that Cadel does not need to win a second Tour to prove that his first in 2011 was not just a flash in the pan. Backing his position is a career record that started with an eighth on debut in 2005, fourth in 2006, and then seconds in 2007 and 2008 before falling way short in 2009 and 2010 and bouncing back with his 2011 triumph. His record and the way he won the Tour cements his credibility as a truly worthy winner.

There is no question that his team was good, but there were a couple of moments, such as the stage to Galibier and the climb up l'Alpe d'Huez, where he was in a good position thanks to his team but still had to finish the job on his own two legs; this was particularly true in the Grenoble time trial.

But what truly vindicated the victory was that he won the Tour after he had been twice second, once fourth and had two blips, and had also performed so well in the other races—coming fifth in the Giro and the 2009 world title showed he wasn't way off.

Before the 2011 Tour many felt that Cadel was no longer a contender. But by the time he reached Paris in the yellow jersey, he had established himself as a most worthy Tour champion—and the second-oldest Tour winner. But most importantly, and no matter how many more Tour titles he wins, Cadel's place in cycling history—the first Australian to ever win the Tour—is his forever. No-one can ever take that from him.

ACKNOWLEDGEMENTS

Without a doubt, a huge thanks goes to Cadel himself for winning the Tour and giving us all so much joy, and for his time over the years in giving interviews and insights into what goes on in the peloton—through the highs and lows. And of course, a huge thanks goes to the team around Cadel that has supported and assisted me—from his wife, Chiara Passerini, who has stood by him through all the highs and lows and his Australian agent Jason Bakker, who must wonder how his life has changed in the last 12 months, to those on the BMC team. My gratitude goes to BMC owner Andy Rihs, president Jim Ochowicz, John Lelangue, Georges Luechinger, George Hincapie, Brent Bookwalter and everyone at BMC who gave their time and thoughts. I would also like to pass on a huge thank-you to photographer Graham Watson, a very dear friend who probably sees more of Cadel from behind his lens by following him in races on a motor bike than anyone I know, and whose insights into Cadel over a fine wine or two were invaluable.

It would be remiss not to recognise the *Sydney Morning Herald* for backing me in covering the sport—in particular, the Tour. To publisher and editor-in-chief Peter Fray and Editor Amanda Wilson at the 'pointy' end of the paper: thanks for seeing that the Tour is not just a sports story, but a truly great news story too, and for giving it the coverage it deserves.

I am also indebted to the *Sydney Morning Herald* sports department. It was Ian Fuge, the managing sports editor, who had the great foresight to rubber-stamp our extended coverage of cycling, in particular the Tour. It was Ian who went in to bat for me and came back with his huge, infectious Welsh grin and said: 'Rupe ... we're doing it. You're going to the Tour.' Ian, your support and vision to follow the cycling path editorially as we do now was brave and bold—Chapeau! Ditto to our online sports editor Stephen Samuelson, who has been right behind me, and to the paper's sports editor Ben Coady, deputy sports editor Kathryn Wicks, Sun-Herald sports editor Paul Suttor and the entire desk ... many, many thanks. Sorry if my typos, grammar and sentence structure have caused you grief.

Thanks too, to my travelling partners from *Velo News* (USA)—past and present—for your help and for the laughs, especially my long-time 'hombre' Andy Hood, who somehow puts up with me not being able to drive. Ditto to John Wilcockson, who first opened the door for me to cover the sport in Europe in 1987 when I joined *Winning* magazine and later became the European correspondent for *Velo News* (USA).

And to all of my friends and colleagues on the European circuit, thanks for the friendship and the help over the years. Gold star to Gregor Brown for his support during proofing as we followed the Giro d'Italia. The same goes to the increasing Australian press corps on the Tour: the camaraderie is growing by the year, as is Australian cycling!

And of course there is the Hardie Grant team who has put the hard yards into publishing this book. To Managing Director Julie Pinkham, Publisher Pam Brewster, editor Jane Thompson, project manager Brooke Clarke and cover designer Josh Durham, thanks for allowing me to work on this project and for your input. And thanks, as always, to my agent, Margaret Gee, for your support and advice; and to Lesley Williamson for her quick, neat and time-saving transcriptions of my interviews with people I spoke to for this book.

I'd like to thank my cycling family—Frank Conceicao, Colin Ironmonger and all the crew at the Eastern Suburbs Cycling Club in Sydney, who remind me why we love the sport in the first place—to ride and enjoy riding.

As always, I am indebted to my family and friends—especially to my wife, Libby, mother, Daphne, step-mother, Consuelo, and the two who are no longer with us but are sorely missed, my father, Perry and step-father, Robin. Without all of you, it simply couldn't be done.

Finally, to you, the reader: thank you. I hope you find this book treats Cadel's story justly, and at the same time provides the sort of insight you wanted into what it takes to win the Tour. It's your passion for the sport that keeps cycling thriving. May it long continue ...

Rupert Guinness